Dearest Angel

By
Elaine Cochrane Murphy

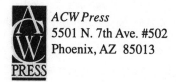
ACW Press
5501 N. 7th Ave. #502
Phoenix, AZ 85013

Publisher's Cataloging-in-Publication
(Provided by Quality Books, Inc.)

Murphy, Elaine Cochrane, 1940-
　　　Dearest angel / by Elaine Cochrane Murphy — 1st ed.
　　　p. cm.
　　　ISBN 1-892525-02-X

　　　1. Cochrane, John F., 1941-1966 2. Vietnamese
Conflict, 1961-1975--Biography. 3. United States. Army
--Biography. 4. Soldiers--United States--Biography.
I. Title

U53.C63M87 1999　　　　　959.704'3'092 [B]
　　　　　　　　　　　　　　QBI98-1414

Printed in the United States of America

To obtain more copies please contact:
Elaine Cochrane Murphy
P.O. Box 135
Patton, CA 92369
See the order form in the back of this book.

Dedication

To my brother,
David William Foster,
Vietnam veteran

Contents

JOHN

I saw him first in April
When they said, "You have a boy."
I waited long to hear these words,
So he became my joy.

And every time his birthday came
I saw him growing tall.
And then he started off to school
In just no time at all.

It seemed I only turned around
And he was in his teens.
He went around in funny hats
And had his favorite jeans.

Then track and football filled his life;
His high school days were fun.
And in his private treasure box
Went medals that he'd won.

And often when he came back home
From being on a date,
He'd whisper at my bedroom door,
"Mom, are you still awake?"

Then we would talk a little while
Before he went to bed.
And I would often breathe a prayer
"God bless my son," I said.

I saw him last in April when he said,
"Mom, don't you worry.
I'm leaving now for Vietnam—
We'll win this in a hurry."

But he will nevermore be back,
My heart still seems to break.
I'll never hear him whisper now,
"Mom, are you still awake?"

Yet I thank God for every joy,
For all the love and fun.
And locked in my heart's treasure box
Are memories of my son.

Muriel Cochrane

An Introduction

It was Monday morning, October 24, 1966, and fall was in the air. I was barely awake that morning, but my thoughts immediately drifted to my husband, John. I hadn't seen him for six months, but in six days we would be together again. I glanced at the airline ticket and hotel reservation on my dresser. The new clothes I had purchased were ready to be packed—the open suitcase was on the floor. I tried to picture John; I could almost feel his strong arms around me. Soon I would leave California to meet him in Hawaii where we would bask in the warm tropical sun and feel the white sand beneath our feet. It was so close now; nothing would keep us apart. Just five more days and a wake up call; then we would be together for five wonderful and glorious days.

The sound of the alarm brought me back to reality. It was a work day, and I needed to be up. My twin sister, Emily, had just moved home from Texas the day before, and we made arrangements to have lunch together. I planned to pick her up at noon, have lunch, and then take her back with me to Norton Air Force Base to visit some of her friends. We had always been close, and I was glad she was home.

The morning zipped by quickly, and before I knew it, I was on my way home to pick up Emily. As I turned the corner by my house, I noticed an unfamiliar blue car parked across the street. The Army sticker on the back bumper caught my attention. My head started to spin as I pulled into the driveway. Why was that car here? Were they seeing our neighbors? I sat in the car afraid to move. In a few moments my sister came out of the house. She walked over to the car.

"There's someone here to see you," she said in a quiet voice.

"Is it about John," I asked.

She looked down and nodded yes. I knew, in that moment, what had happened, but forced myself to ask her the question I had never wanted to say.

"Has John been. . . killed?"

"He asked me not to say anything," she answered, but as she spoke she shook her head yes. I stepped out of the car, and we walked toward the house. My body was starting to shake, and I didn't know if I could handle what I was about to hear. There had to be some mistake; in six days we'd be together again. And besides, I had just received a letter from him.

He was a tall Army officer, a first lieutenant, the same rank as John. He stood to his feet as I entered the room, and I will never forget his words.

"I've come to give you the worst possible news. Your husband, 1st Lt. John Cochrane, was killed this morning, October 24, 1966, in Vietnam by a sniper's bullet." He offered his condolences, said I would be contacted very shortly by Army officials to make final arrangements, and then within a few short minutes was gone. His job was completed, but my life would never be the same.

1
Off to Japan

I met John three and half years earlier, in April 1963, in Tokyo, Japan. Emily and I were selected to spend one year in Tokyo working for Youth With a Mission (YWAM). This interdenominational organization sent youth to work in foreign countries to assist missionaries with secular work so that they could focus on the work God had called them to do. I was assigned to work for the Chairman of the Assemblies of God Headquarters, and Emily worked for the Director of the Far East Broadcasting Company. We would both be doing secretarial work.

I remember getting off the plane in Tokyo on that September night of 1962. We were the last passengers off and were carrying so much luggage we could barely move. The Hulet family, our initial contact in Tokyo, finally found us, and we were soon on our way to their house driving on the "wrong" side of the road. Tokyo was an enormous city with ten million people—much different than our small hometown of San Bernardino, California. Within the next several days, Mr. Hulet gave us a tour of the city. But he cautioned us that Tokyo was so big, we'd never see it in the one year we would be there. There was a lot of construction as Tokyo prepared for the upcoming Olympics, and the heat and dust, added to the humidity, made for some uncomfortable days.

We lived temporarily with the Hulet family until our own housing was arranged. Mr. Hulet, Emily's boss, lived in a lovely home in Tokyo. When entering their house, you removed your shoes and put on a pair of slippers. I liked that tradition, and we decided to continue with it when we moved to our own place. We lived at the Hulet's home for one month and have fond memories of our stay with them. Living with Mr. & Mrs. Hulet was their teenage daughter Robin, and their Japanese maid Mitsaka. Mitsaka was a great cook, and I remember eating breakfast with the family around the table each morning. We had our own special place mats and napkin rings—and oh, the great cinnamon rolls she made! We sure missed those when we moved to our own place.

We eventually located our own American/Japanese-style house and moved in on October 15, 1962. It was a small place, but it had all the essentials: one bedroom, one bath, a kitchen, and living room. One very distinctive element we loved was a Japanese sunken bath. However, being close to train tracks was a challenge, and our small home vibrated each time a train flew by. Our first few nights were rather sleepless as we were sure a train was about to crash through our house. We eventually grew accustomed to the noise and the vibration and were able to sleep through the night with no disturbance.

We also had to adjust to living on our own in a foreign country. We had to do all of our shopping though we knew very little Japanese. We could say, "How much," "Yes," "No," "Good morning," "Good evening," and "How are you?" But that was about the extent of our vocabulary. I remember trying to talk to the man who brought our heating oil. When he said "takai," we thought he was talking about how "high" the price of heating oil was, but he was actually commenting on how tall we were. And then the word "hi," which actually means "yes" in Japanese, created a problem. We thought the clerks at the stores were really friendly, greeting us with a "hi," but they were actually saying, "Yes, may we help you?"

I remember becoming very homesick soon after we moved into our own place. I'd take my airline ticket out and think, *It sure would be nice to be home.* I missed my family and friends and wondered how we would manage one whole year away from home.

We soon settled into a routine. Having no car, we depended totally on the trains, subways, and taxicabs. I took the train to work every morning, while Emily rode the train and then transferred to the subway. It was always an ordeal riding a subway—especially during the early morning rush hours. The train companies employed university students to push as many people into the subway cars as possible. We felt like sardines in a can! However, Emily and I had an advantage; we were both 5'8", and we had plenty of breathing room above the crowds. We laughed a lot those first few weeks as we grew accustomed to a whole new way of living.

We lived close to the Grant Heights housing area where Air Force families lived. We attended services at the chapel and were able to meet some American people. It was refreshing to hear a language we understood.

We ate Thanksgiving dinner at a church in the Tachikawa area, and then several members took food to the nearby Leper Colony. That was quite an experience! I remember accidentally dropping my pumpkin pie on the floor and feeling very embarrassed. The missionary said it was good that it happened because it immediately put the lepers at ease. Seeing someone with two perfectly good hands drop something made them feel less clumsy.

Letters and news from California were always a welcome relief. Emily and I met each day at the Ikebukaro Train Station after work for the ride back to Narimasu Station. We would read the mail on the way home; it always brightened our day.

We spent Christmas with the Hulet family. That Christmas morning was very cold, and we were surprised to hear a knock on our bedroom door. The house-girl delivered two glasses of warm milk that helped us deal with the numbing temperatures of the small unattached room where we were sleeping. It was nice being with a family during the holidays, but this was our first Christmas away from home, and our thoughts were back home in California. Our mom sent a couple of songs by Elvis to cheer us up: "I'll be Home for Christmas," and "It'll be a Blue Christmas Without You." Boy, did that bring tears to our eyes! Oh well, only nine more months, and we'd be on our way home.

Before we knew it, we were into a new year. It was 1963, and the months began to pass quickly. One of our girlfriends from California, Jan Curtis, flew over to see us in March. It was good to see her again. It was a great experience walking down the street—Jan with her beautiful flaming red hair, Emily, a blonde, and me with my brown hair. We received quite a few looks and comments as we passed by, but we had fun with it. Jan was in no hurry to get back home to the States, so she decided to stay on for a few more months.

Shortly after Jan arrived, our pastor and his wife from California came to visit and do some ministering. We joined them on a short vacation to Kobe and ended up staying in

an orphanage there. This was a memorable time as we saw
more of Japan as well as the precious orphans who were
taken care of so lovingly by the missionaries.

We had been in Japan for several months when I wrote
the following poem that described our mission:

> To the Orient we have traveled,
> Across islands, sea, and sky.
> To a heathen land bound in sin,
> Where we hear the millions cry.
>
> Our mother and dad we bade good-bye
> Our sister and brothers, too.
> For awaiting us on the other shore
> Was a job that we had to do.
>
> Under Youth With a Mission we were to go,
> One year of our lives to give;
> Not by might nor by power
> But by His Spirit we would live.
>
> Many months have passed us by
> Since the day we boarded the plane.
> Many souls we've helped to tell,
> Of a heaven they could gain.
>
> Our time will soon be finished
> In this land of the Rising Sun.
> But many memories we will have
> Of God's work that was done.

My twin sister Emily, Jan Curtis, and me in
Tokyo, May 1963

2
John

It was an April evening in 1963 when I first met John F. Cochrane. Earlier in the week, Emily met a young man on the train by the name of Jim Dobbs. He introduced himself, and during the conversation, she told him about our work with YWAM and the one year commitment we made to serve in Tokyo. Since we were involved in Christian work, he wanted to introduce us to two soldiers who were new in the country and who were both Preachers' Kids (P.K.s). He made arrangements for us to meet the following Saturday night following a Sayonara Party that Emily, Jan, and I were planning to attend at Grant Heights Chapel. We would meet them at the snack bar following the party.

However, the party lasted longer than we had anticipated. Suddenly, someone gave us a message that three men were asking for us outside. They had waited for us at the snack bar until it closed. John told me later he was embarrassed about coming to the Chapel, and if it would have been up to him, they never would have shown up, though I'm certainly glad they didn't listen to him.

The first thing Jim said when we walked outside was, "These two guys are "P.K.s." My ears immediately perked up as I had always wanted to be a preacher's wife, but if that didn't work out, marrying a preacher's kid was next best. He introduced them as John Cochrane from Michigan and Howard Prough from Florida. They were both attractive, but when John smiled I noticed a gap between his front teeth. It didn't take away from his looks, but rather added to his boyish appearance. We ended up going to Jim's house and talked till late at night. John and Howard had great personalities and kept us laughing most of the time. Emily and I made plans to meet them for chapel service the next morning at the Narimasu train station by our house and then take a taxi to the chapel. Emily and I were late, and as we walked up we could see Howard nervously looking at his watch and pacing back and forth. John, however, looked calm and had one foot resting on a railing as he smoked a pipe.

We made arrangements with them to go out for dinner one evening, and they planned to pick us up and take a taxi to the restaurant. We chatted for a few minutes at our house first, and then Emily, John, and Howard went ahead while I put on my shoes. I heard someone waiting outside the door and wondered if it was John or Howard. When I finally finished with my shoes, I found John patiently waiting for me. I liked him. Hmmm...maybe he liked me, too.

A few weeks went by, and I didn't hear from John. *Why hasn't he called? Maybe he didn't like me as much as I liked him*, I thought. I decided to take a chance and give him a call. What would one call matter anyway? I dialed the number for his squadron at the Army post and asked to speak to him. He was playing pool, so it took him quite awhile to get to the phone. After we exchanged hellos and some small talk, he asked, "By the way, who is this?" I said, "How many American girls do you know in Tokyo?" We ended up making a date for the following Saturday night to ride the train downtown to the Ginza, have dinner, and then do some window shopping. Of course, my very favorite food was sukiyaki, so there was no question where we would eat.

We chatted during the train ride and got to know each other a little bit better. We had a lot in common.

We both came from Christian homes and had accepted the Lord as Savior at a young age. We both came from families with five children. John had four sisters and was the only son, and I had two brothers and two sisters (one being my twin sister, Emily, who is my older sister by 22 minutes. We were actually triplets when we were born, but the third was a boy who was stillborn.) John had a very strong Christian upbringing and was grounded in the Word, and I liked that. His father was an evangelist and traveled quite extensively stateside and overseas with Youth for Christ, and when he was away on evangelistic crusades, his mom kept the home fires burning.

After a delicious sukiyaki dinner and a stroll on the Ginza hand in hand, we rode the train home and then took a taxi to my house. I invited him in, and we talked some more. In the middle of our conversation, sitting in the kitchen, he pulled me close to him, put his arms around me, and gave me a big kiss. I liked that! When he left, there was a gentle rain falling outside. He told me later he didn't need an umbrella to shield him from the rain because he "floated" all the way back to the barracks.

I continued working at the Assemblies of God Headquarters, but my health began to deteriorate. I was losing weight and battling severe nausea. Finally, the doctors decided to hospitalize me to run some tests. I spent several days in the hospital, but still they were unable to diagnose my condition, and I wasn't getting better. I was finally discharged from the hospital and went to stay with my boss' family. I remember being on the couch in the living room most of the time and feeling emotionally drained. I would cry over anything. I felt a great fear taking hold of my life. I thought I had a horrible disease and was going to die.

The missionaries had a meeting and decided it would be best to return me to the States for further medical help. I was feeling worse every day, and even though they prayed for me, I continued to lose weight, experience waves of nausea, and feelings of hopelessness.

The decision was made, and I was going home. As sick as I was, I felt enormously sad. I made a commitment to work for YWAM for one year and now would be going home three months early. I didn't want to leave Emily behind. What would happen to our little house; what would happen to my job? What would happen to me?

It also meant I would be leaving John, and I didn't want to leave him. I liked him; I liked him a lot. We had shared many hours together talking about our past, our present situation, and our lives together in the future. Would this be the end of our relationship? We had dated for only a short time, and we kept telling each other this was only a platonic relationship, but I knew better. Did God bring us together? Was John the one God had for me? We discussed the situation at length, and decided if God wanted us together, He would make a way. We would leave it in His hands. So that he wouldn't forget me, I gave him a thin gold chain with a small amethyst stone which I always wore. I put it around his neck, and he promised he wouldn't take it off until he saw me again. That made me feel good.

Emily and Jan packed up our things in the little house. The decision was made that Emily would move in with the Hymes family and continue working my job at Headquarters. It had been about three months since Jan arrived, and she decided it was time for her to move on. It was hard saying goodbye to everyone, but I promised I would keep in touch by mail. Jan and I boarded the plane in Tokyo on June 22, 1963. I didn't know if I would see any of my friends again. I was sick, and I hoped and prayed someone could help me. Jan would fly as far as Hawaii and then take a plane to Samoa to visit missionary friends. I would continue home to California.

When we landed in Hawaii, I ordered a tall, cold glass of milk. I missed milk the most in Japan. I also liked pineapple, and since it was so plentiful in Hawaii, I sat down to an order of pineapple slices and a glass of cold milk. The combination might not sound appetizing, but it tasted delicious. I told Jan good-bye as she boarded the plane for Samoa. In five hours I would be landing at Los Angeles International Airport. My parents and my brother Chuck and his family would meet me at the plane. It would be good to be home again and with family who loved me.

My parents immediately made an appointment for me at Loma Linda University Medical Center to see a doctor who specialized in Oriental diseases. After many tests, I was diagnosed with "tropical sprue," a malabsorption syndrome affecting the intestinal tract. The treatment was Vitamin B-12 shots, which I began immediately.

Over the summer months, I gradually began to recover physically, but mentally and emotionally I was not doing well. I was suffering from depression and oppression, and fear had filled my mind. As a Christian, I knew we were engaged in spiritual warfare with an enemy named Satan who was out to steal, kill and destroy us. But there were many thoughts flooding my mind; i.e., *I wasn't born again or a child of God, I had a horrible disease and was going to die,* thoughts of losing my mind and that, perhaps, I had committed an unpardonable sin. I didn't realize these weren't my own thoughts, but lies from Satan, yet I took them in, dwelled on them, and they became strongholds in my life. If Satan can get us to believe his lies, he can control our lives. I knew God had provided victory for us as His children, but I didn't know how to experience it. I felt as if I was caught in quicksand and couldn't get free.

My parents took me to see a friend of theirs who was a psychiatrist, and he immediately prescribed tranquilizers. These helped ease the pain, but the thoughts wouldn't go away, and I couldn't get relief from the fear. A list of how I felt included despair, blackness, hopelessness, agony, being overwhelmed, guilty, doubtful, phobic, having panic attacks, and agoraphobic (which made me a prisoner in my own home). I was tormented. I had no joy, no peace, no happiness. I prayed, but it seemed my prayers bounced off the ceiling. I couldn't sense God's presence, and I thought He had left me. I felt so alone.

I have learned many lessons and realized many truths since that time. God was definitely with me through those years even though I couldn't sense His presence. He said He would never leave me nor forsake me, but I was going by my feelings, and feelings have nothing to do with faith. Faith is taking God at His Word, believing what He said no matter what our five senses tell us, and standing up to walk in the victory that is ours.

There was one daily ray of sunshine when the mailman stopped in front of our house, and, if I saw John's handwriting on an envelope, I was transformed. He was a great letter writer and could make even dull news sound exciting. In one letter he talked about coming to California in October for a visit. Of course I wrote back and told him how great it would be to see him again. I didn't want to sound too excited, but my pulse quickened every time I thought about his visit.

3
Elopement

John made arrangements for a flight home. My sister, Emily had returned from Japan, and we were scheduled to speak at a church in Yucca Valley. I planned to pick up John at the Burbank Airport and drive immediately to the church. It was so great seeing him again, and we talked non-stop all the way to the church. I told him I would be sharing some of my experiences in Japan, and I remember him saying, "Just make me proud." The service went well, and it was fun remembering and talking about the many good things that happened while we were with YWAM. We drove back home after the service and stayed up late talking.

John and I spent time talking, shopping, and eating out. Then we would talk some more. Somehow, the word marriage kept creeping into the conversation. We made arrangements to have dinner at the Sycamore Inn, which was a great place to eat. More than that, it was a romantic restaurant with dimmed lights and soft music—the perfect place—the perfect atmosphere! Actually, John didn't have to say anything because I knew this was the night he would ask, and when he did I said, "Yes, I will be your wife, and, yes, I will follow you wherever the Army sends you even to the ends of the earth." He slipped the ring on my finger, a beautiful and simple solitaire ring.

But when? I had always wanted a big church wedding, but John would only be in California a few more days, so that was out of the question. And money—well, we didn't have much of that either. But we did come up with a solution...we would drive to Las Vegas, get secretly married, and then save our money for a big wedding in the spring. On Wednesday morning, October 15, 1963, we put our wedding clothes in my little blue VW and headed for Las Vegas. John would wear his navy blue suit which was tailor-made in Japan, and I would wear my turquoise blue Lily Rubin suit. We told my parents we were going to visit John's cousin near Santa Barbara. (Be sure your sins will find you out.)

We drove up and down the boulevard in Las Vegas until we found just the right chapel, which turned out to be The Little White Chapel. Before we got out of the car, John said, "Let's pray about this. If it's the Lord's will, everything will work out. If not, it will be blocked in some way." So, we held hands, and John led us in a short and simple prayer. When we went inside and inquired about getting married, we discovered we didn't have enough money to cover the cost. We looked at each other, walked outside, got into our car and said, "That's it. The Lord must not want us to get married now."

Just as we were getting ready to leave, one of the ladies came out and asked John if he was in the military. When he said yes, she said, "In that case, you can go ahead and get married, pay what you can now, and send the rest of the money later." We just looked at each other and smiled. The Lord knew we wanted to get married, and He had worked it out. We proceeded to change into our wedding attire, and I walked down the short aisle to the tune of the Hawaiian Wedding Song (my favorite). We both said, "I do," and were pronounced Mr. & Mrs. John F. Cochrane. We then sat down on the front pew and listened to a recording of the vows we had just taken. It brought tears to my eyes. I couldn't believe we really did it; I mean, without a relative or friend in sight and no one else to share in our joy.

We drove back to San Bernardino after the ceremony. The chapel had given us a newlywed packet containing soap, aspirin, etc., and, not wanting to reveal our secret, we quickly disposed of the "evidence." We only shared the news with my two sisters, Emily and Margie. Of course, they were totally shocked, but said they wouldn't breathe a word to anyone. We felt certain no one would learn about it.

In a few short days, John was gone. I drove him to the Burbank Airport, and we said our goodbyes. It was hard to see him go, but I knew spring would be here soon. I had lots of planning to do for the big wedding, and I needed time to make all the arrangements. John planned to visit the Personnel Office at the army post to make a change in his status. He now had a dependent wife and that would add a few more dollars to his paycheck. Any additional money would help us. I was sure a big wedding would be expensive.

About a week later I got a job at Aerospace Corporation, and soon thereafter received a call from Emily. "Mom knows you and John are married, and she's very upset." I couldn't believe what I was hearing. I wondered how in the world she found out. I hung up in total shock. Now I would have to go home and face my parents alone. If only John were with me, it would make it so much easier. I delayed going home as long as I could; it was dark by the time I walked through the back door. Mom was sitting at the kitchen table reading the newspaper. I tried to walk by quietly, but then I heard, "Well, Mrs. Cochrane." I answered, "Well, Mrs. Foster," as I proceeded to the living room with Mom close on my heels. Margie was sitting in the living room, and as we began the conversation, she immediately spoke up on my behalf. What we did seemed perfectly logical to her, and she let my mom know. (My sisters were great; they were the only ones we confided in, and I knew they had kept our secret.)

My parents were both extremely hurt, not that we had gotten married, but the way we went about it. One of our neighbors saw our names (John Cochrane and Elaine Foster) in the newspaper under the heading "Marriage Licenses Issued in Las Vegas." The neighbor called my mom to see if John and I had indeed gotten married while he was home on leave. Of course, my mom knew nothing about it, and was shocked when she looked at the newspaper herself. We had no idea our newspaper routinely published the names of those taking out marriage licenses in Las Vegas, but my brother Chuck, who worked for the County of San Bernardino, said he was aware of the procedure. The secret was out, and so was the big wedding in the spring. I canceled the engagement picture that was to run in the local newspaper and changed it to a wedding announcement instead. John and I both felt very badly about how the whole situation turned out. As he stated in a letter to my folks, he wouldn't change anything except to have had our parents standing by our sides, and I agreed with him totally.

October 1963

Dear Mr. & Mrs. Foster:

This letter should have been written quite some time ago, but if you have been reading your papers, you will know that we have been quite busy over here in the Far East. Actually, this letter should never have had to be written. What I have to say should have been said face to face when I was there with you. Had I faced up to my responsibilities as both a husband and a man, many hurt feelings would have been spared.

Since receiving Elaine's letter explaining how you learned of our marriage, I have been trying to think what I would or could say to make things easier for both of us. However, I know that there is nothing that I can say that will erase the hurt you must have felt when you found out. I cannot honestly say that I am sorry we did what we did because I love Elaine more than anything on this earth. However, I do humbly ask your forgiveness for the way we went about it; and for not telling you.

There were several times after we were married when I wanted to tell you, but never did. As you might have guessed, my moonlight walk in the orange groves was due to struggling with what I should tell you. And on the last day, when you gave me the money, I felt like the lowest form of life on this earth, and I almost ran to the kitchen and spilled the whole story. However, I kept telling myself that there was no way you would find out, and it would just cause friction between us. Had I only known then what I know now, I would have gladly told you and faced the consequences.

It might also interest you to know that I have written my parents and told them all about it. They, too, will be hurt and disappointed, not so much because I got married, but because I did so without their knowledge or presence.

I am looking forward to the time when I can come home again, and I am in hopes of mending any fences that may be damaged because of what Elaine and I did. This may seem strange to you, but in the short time I have known you, I have come to love and respect you both for many things and in many ways. I would hate to see any growing animosity come between us because of what has happened.

In closing, I would like to say that if I could undo all that's happened during the past month, the only change I would make would be to have both of our parents beside us when we were married.

I remain respectfully yours,

J.

Here is a portion of the letter John sent to his parents in Michigan:

Dear Parents:

What I have to tell you will be somewhat of a shock. However, as a family we have been through quite a lot in the last few years, and I feel that I am doing the right thing in telling you now rather than later. Elaine and I were married in Las Vegas, Nevada, the 15th of October. We were married by a Baptist preacher in a very quiet, but wonderful ceremony. We took off for Las Vegas on Wednesday morning at 0700 hours. The trip was uneventful except that we both kept shaking like leaves. When we finally got there, we ate lunch and then went to a very pretty wedding chapel. Then I did a strange thing. I bowed my head and prayed out loud. In the course of the prayer, I asked the Lord to have His way in this big decision of our lives. When we raised our heads, and this is the truth, we were both steady as a rock.

I asked the lady at the desk what it cost to get married. Including the license, the total cost was $20, and with that she gave us the directions to city hall to get our license. Elaine and I conferred for a moment and found out that we had only $20.75 between us, and we needed gas to get back to her house. We told the lady we thought that we would wait for awhile and went outside to the car. We sat there for a few minutes and talked. We remembered what I said about "God's Will." Just as I was about to drive away, the lady came out and asked if we were short on cash, and I said, "Yes, we are." She then asked if I was in the service, and I said "Yes" again, but I haven't the slightest idea how she knew that. She then said that if we still wanted to get married that we could pay her $10, get the license for $5, and that would leave us $5 to get back home. We talked it over and decided to go ahead with the wedding plans. We changed clothes and had the ceremony, which was perfect. So that was about the way it happened. We then changed clothes again and headed back for San Bernardino.

I hope that you will understand why we got married, and that it was for no malicious reasons against either of our parents. I love you both very much and truly regret that this might hurt you. For the hurt I have caused, I ask your forgiveness, and for our marriage I ask your blessing because it means much to me. I remain yours respectively,

Your son,

J.

I changed my name legally, started wearing my wedding ring, and looked forward to a long and happy married life. I continued working at Aerospace Corporation and made plans to return to Japan in the spring. It would be good to be with John again.

It was our first Christmas as husband and wife, and we would have to spend it apart. John sent a beautiful strand of pearls with matching earrings and a Christmas card with the following message:

My Dearest Wife:

Tradition has it that Christmas is a time of joy and giving, and what better time could I have picked than at Christmas to express the joy and love you have bestowed upon me since becoming my wife. With this small present I wish to give you a symbol of my love and affection. I sincerely hope that our love may grow and become "perfect" even as the most expensive pearls should be.

When you wear them, think not only of their beauty, but also of the love I have for you which they represent.

I love you,

J

I had a husband who loved me, a job I enjoyed, and a family who supported me in every way. In spite of all this, I continued to experience moments of fear and anxiety. I went to work, to church, and maintained a normal life, but inside I wasn't free. I was a child of God, but I couldn't sense His presence. I was living on feelings instead of faith, and that kept me defeated instead of victorious. When would I be free again inside? I would continue suffering in quiet desperation for many years, but freedom would eventually come.

4

Army Life

I returned to Japan in May of 1964. John was at the airport to meet me, and as I walked off the plane I could see him patiently waiting for me. He met me at the baggage claim area with a big hug and kiss. It felt good to be with him again. We took a taxi to the hotel in downtown Tokyo. This would be our first night together, and after being separated for seven months, we were both rather nervous. Shortly after we arrived in the room, the telephone rang. It was one of John's buddies from his squadron at the Post. Of course he wanted to know how things were going and what we were doing. John told him it was none of his business as he laughed and hung up the phone. The next morning I was awakened by horns honking, brakes squealing, and loud voices from the street far below. A big city has different smells and sounds, and I knew I was back in Tokyo.

We took a taxi to the house that John rented for us, and I was surprised to find it was in the very same area where Emily and I lived a year earlier. The furniture he scraped together left a lot to be desired. The bed didn't have a box spring and was not that comfortable, but we didn't care. We were newlyweds, and as long as we were together, nothing else mattered.

We bought an old Chevrolet, and I actually got up the nerve to drive in the big city and in real traffic. It took me awhile to get accustomed to driving on the opposite side of the road; I had to keep saying to myself, "stay to the left".

Driving or riding in Tokyo took nerves of steel especially in a taxi cab. We would get in, close our eyes, and hang on for dear life. We always gave a sigh of relief as we paid the driver and exited the taxi in one piece. Our guardian angels were riding with us, and we were forever grateful.

John and I were in Japan only two months when he received orders to report to Fort Benning, Georgia, to attend Officer Candidate School (OCS). Training would begin the middle of August. We made preparations to return to the States by the end of July. John had applied for OCS so it looked like we were headed in the right direction. When we returned home from Japan, we decided to drive across country to Fort Benning by way of John's hometown, Dearborn, Michigan. That way we would be able to visit John's family and see some of the country at the same time. We invited John's cousin, Tim Postiff, to accompany us on the trip so that I wouldn't be driving alone on the return trip to California.

It was extremely hot the night we left San Bernardino. We wanted to get across the desert during the coolest part of the day, but I remember the stifling heat. The air was so heavy we could barely breathe. We drove to the Grand Canyon and grabbed a few winks of sleep in sleeping bags stretched out on the ground. The Grand Canyon is an awesome sight! I wondered how anyone could not believe in a Supreme Being after seeing that magnificent view.

We finally made it to Columbus, Georgia, home of Fort Benning. This is where John would spend the next six months in rigorous training to become an officer in the U.S. Army. John liked the Army, and I'm sure had thoughts of making it his career. He had six tough months of training ahead of him, and he could only concentrate on making it through each day and hopefully to graduation. He had dreams of a gold bar pinned on his shoulder.

Tim and I returned to California driving almost non-stop by taking turns driving and sleeping. I decided to get a job while John was at OCS. Six months was a long time to be idle. I applied at Aerospace Corporation and landed a secretarial job within a few days. That meant a little extra money in my pocket and it would also help pass the time.

It was the end of October, and John wanted me to fly down for the weekend to attend a big party hosted by the battalion. I was only able to spend the weekend as John had to be back in training by Monday morning. Even though it was a short time, it was well worth it. I liked being back in John's arms. I felt loved and special. The party at Fort Benning was a big success. I was able to meet some of John's buddies and, of course, his commanding officer. He had some free time for the weekend, so we visited his favorite family restaurant in Columbus where I was treated to peanut butter cream pie. That was his favorite! I had to agree; it was the best peanut butter cream pie I had ever tasted. The weekend was over all too soon, and I was back on the airplane and on my way home before I knew it. I was soon back at work, counting the days until Christmas.

John and three of his OCS buddies drove to California for the holidays. They dropped John off at my house and then proceeded to their own homes in California to spend time with their families. Christmas is my favorite time of the year. John's mom, Muriel, joined us for Christmas that year, so that was an extra special treat. Before we knew it, it was time for John to make the return trip to Fort Benning. It seemed like we were saying "hello" or "goodbye" much too often, but February was just around the corner, and soon we would be able to set up housekeeping permanently.

On February 1, 1965, I packed up our gold Mustang and headed for Georgia. My Grandpa Nash gave me some parting advice. "Don't pick up any hitchhikers, even if they're women." He didn't have to worry. My car was so loaded, front and back, that I didn't have an inch of space to spare. I drove to Apache Junction, Arizona, the first day and spent the night with a long-time missionary friend, Esther Treece. She and her husband had been missionaries to the Apache Indians, and her husband had recently passed away. It was good to spend some time visiting with her. Missionaries are a special group of people who make many sacrifices to help get the gospel to the ends of the earth such as leaving family behind, and forfeiting the comforts and conveniences of home. It seems there should be a special reward in heaven for the many missionaries who have given their lives for the sake of the gospel.

It was Friday morning, February 5th, when I finally arrived at Fort Benning. My trip was uneventful, but I did find truth to the saying, "Texas was miles and miles of nothing but miles and miles." It was a beautiful state, but long to get across. I tried to call John all along the way, but the telephone was always busy, busy, busy, and I never was able to get through to him. I found out later that it was the one phone used by everyone in the platoon. I went immediately to the Commander's office and introduced myself, and he asked me to have a seat while he sent word to John to report to his office. In a very short time, John came walking through the door, his face a rather ashen color. Since John hadn't heard from me all week, he had visions of me being in a car wreck splattered across some highway along the way. He was extremely relieved when he saw me stand-ing there in one piece. After saluting the Commander, John was dismissed from his office, and we were finally together again.

Graduation day came on February 15, 1965, and it was one happy day for all of the men in the 52nd Officer Candidate Company. John's platoon leader wrote the following message to his men:

Men of the 1st Platoon:

For the past twenty three weeks you have been through one of the more difficult schools that the Army has to offer. You have felt mental and physical pressure, meeting it head-on, and through sheer determination overcame these necessary obstacles. However, you have only scratched the surface, for OCS is a small integral part of developing a leader. You will find the future tasks greater, with pressure directly proportional, but through this maze of never ending challenges you will gain what no living being can take away from you—an ever increasing volume of self-improvement. In your future leadership roles, keep in mind that a true leader accepts more than his share of the blame, and less than his share of the credit. Best of luck in the future.

C.A. (Lou) Hennies
1st Lt Infantry
Tactical Officer

And some advice from John's Commanding Officer, Lt. Col. Robert B. Nett:

You have experienced, during the past six months, one of the most rigorous, exacting, and demanding leadership courses in our modern Army. You have been tried and tested and found to be true in fundamental knowledge and leadership ability. You have learned the true meaning and importance of honor and integrity and are now on the springboard of a career which will be challenging and one which should provide you with a great deal of personal satisfaction.

As junior leaders and executives within our vast military machine, I am confident that you will serve your country well and honorably in any capacity.

It has been a distinct and singular pleasure to have served as your Commanding Officer, and I sincerely hope that I may again have the pleasure of sharing service with each of you!

This was the end of the rigorous and demanding training John had endured to become an officer in the U. S. Army. He earned the gold bar, and his family and I were very proud of him! He told me that his mom had sent him a scripture verse from Isaiah 43:2 that helped him through the difficult and grueling months: "When you pass through the waters, I will be with you; and through the rivers, they shall not overflow you. When you walk through the fire, you shall not be burned, nor shall the flame kindle upon you." He said that was his motto while at OCS as well as in future assignments.

John received orders to attend the Officer Familiarization Course at Fort Devens, Massachusetts, with a reporting date of mid-March. The class would last approximately four months, so that meant we would be able to watch the countryside come alive with the beautiful colors of spring after the long winter months.

We arrived in Ayer, Massachusetts, and after John checked in at Fort Devens, we immediately began to search for a place to live. It didn't take us long to find one we liked. It was called Stroud Apartments, and we were soon knocking on the door and talking to an elderly lady by the name of Mrs. Stroud. She invited us in and questioned us at great length. Finally she stood up and said, "Okay, I think you will make good tenants. You can rent the apartment." She quickly added, "Oh, by the way, you're not an officer are you? I have enlisted people in the other three apartments, and I'd like to keep it that way." John and I looked at each other rather disappointed. We liked the place and felt that was where the Lord was directing us. John told her he was a second lieutenant, had just graduated from OCS, and would only be at Fort Devens in training for four months. She thought a little while, and then said she was going to make an exception to her rule. We could rent the apartment, but she didn't want John pulling rank on any of her enlisted men in the other three apartments. She didn't have to worry; John wasn't about to pull rank on anyone.

It was raining heavily the day we moved into our upstairs apartment. We quickly became acquainted with our neighbors who were all stationed at Fort Devens. John left early each morning for work and would come home at noon for lunch. Another buddy from Fort Benning, 2nd Lt. John Michael Casey (better known as Ben Casey), became a frequent visitor at our apartment. John became friends with him at OCS and was happy he, too, had been assigned to Fort Devens for training. We occasionally invited the neighbors over to play cards at night. Rook was the name of the game, and John liked to win! Many Saturday nights were wiled away playing Rook as we all tried to beat John. I still have that deck of cards, though it may be short a card or two.

5
Panic

In spite of much happiness, I continued to live in quiet desperation. Fears filled my mind. One fear that continued to nag me was the fear of death. I prayed, but it didn't seem to bring relief. I visited Mrs. Stroud and talked with her at great length. I shared my fears, especially the fear of dying. It was comforting to chat with her. She had lived a long life, and she seemed to possess a lot of wisdom. About the same time I was having all these thoughts of dying, I received a letter from home saying my Grandpa Nash died in California. I remember that night looking up at the heavens filled with millions of bright and twinkling stars and thinking, "Where is my Grandpa tonight?"

John's dad, Jack Cochrane, was a minister, and he planned a short weekend visit with us. It was good seeing him again. He was a man filled with the wisdom of the Word, and could quote verse after verse of the Bible. I remember the verse he shared with me: Psalms 34:4: "I sought the Lord, and He heard me, and delivered me from all of my fears." That was the truth of the Word. Why couldn't I hold onto that promise? Why couldn't I be free from this tormented mind? I still had much to endure before I would be completely free.

John and his dad loved to play golf, so they took advantage of the beautiful golf course and spring weather in Massachusetts to play eighteen holes. I wasn't a great golfer, but I remember one incident when John and I were playing nine holes. We had come up to a body of water, and

John, knowing that I was a novice player, handed me an old, beat up golf ball. I teed the ball up, took one big swing, and over the water sailed my ball. Boy, that felt good! Now it was John's turn. He took his brand new, shiny ball out of his golf bag, teed it up, took a big swing, and into the water it plopped. He won the game, but I never let him forget that particular hole.

In the month of May new life was springing forth in the countryside. The snow and cold of winter were gone, the birds were singing overhead, new leaves were budding on the trees, and flowers were blooming everywhere. This was my favorite time of the year, but I didn't feel the excitement inside. Satan continued to wreak havoc in my life by filling my mind with fears and doubts. I couldn't grab hold of the truth and reality of God's Word that explained how Satan was a defeated foe, and how God had defeated him at the cross 2,000 years ago. It was up to me to stand up and appropriate in my life what God had already provided for me—victory in my life over the enemy of my soul. I felt so overwhelmed, so helpless, as if I was stuck in quicksand and couldn't get free. It seemed the more I struggled to get free, the more stuck I became.

John called my parents in California. He didn't know what else to do to help me, and he thought they might have some ideas. I thought I was losing my mind. And when he shared that with them, they immediately packed up the truck and camper and began the long drive from the west coast to the east coast. My family had always been like that. If you needed them, they were there to help. Five days later they pulled into our driveway at the Stroud Apartments. I was happy to see Emily with them. She had taken a couple weeks off from her job at Norton Air Force Base to be with me.

Emily and I were always close, like good friends. What happened to one of us usually happened to the other. As kids, I fell out of the car while my mom was driving down the highway. We were fighting in the back seat, and one of us hit the door handle and out I went. I was saved by the heavy snowsuit I was wearing, and the Lord protected me from the truck behind us. My mom stopped the car, got out, and saw me running down the side of the road to meet her. The next day Emily fell out of the hay loft with the same minor injuries I had received falling out of the car—a bruised shoulder—and on the same shoulder.

Then there was rheumatic fever. When we were young children, we lived in Medical Lake, Washington, in an area known as the "Rheumatic Fever Belt." Numerous lakes created a damp climate. Soon I started showing symptoms—tired and lethargic— with nodules that looked like bruises covering my legs. My parents took me to the doctor, and I was diagnosed with rheumatic fever. I was hospitalized in Spokane 18 miles from home. My parents would come to visit as often as they could, but for a six-year old child, it wasn't often enough. After awhile I became homesick and was eating less and less. Finally, the doctors told my parents that unless they brought Emily into the hospital to be with me, I might die of loneliness. Emily also was diagnosed with rheumatic fever, as well as my older brother Chuck, but their illnesses were not as severe as mine.

It was a happy day when Emily came to join me. We were in the same room and we each had our own bed. I remember one rather stern nurse, and we could always tell when she was coming down the hall—as we heard her shoes clicking against the floor. If it was nap time, we'd always close our eyes and pretend we were sleeping. Then there were all the penicillin shots; our backsides must have looked like pin cushions! We were soon discharged to a convalescent home where we spent a few months before finally going home. That was a happy day—to be back home with our family and sleeping in our own beds. We continued as outpatients, and Mom drove us to Spokane for routine check-ups with Dr. Fisher. I remember him as an older doctor with a deep voice. We hated the blood tests and would argue about who was going to get stuck first. The doctor noted that Emily and I always had the same sedimentation rates and the same pulse rates. In fact, all of the tests had identical results which was quite unusual.

Then there was the incident where I almost died from a large loss of blood. I woke up one morning to find blood all over my pillow. My mom cleaned me up, put me on the living room couch, and went to get a doctor. Since we lived in the country and had no telephone, it took awhile for them to return. In the meantime, I continued to spit up clots of blood. The doctor checked me over and said he didn't know where the blood was coming from— perhaps my tonsils. He told my parents to watch me carefully. The blood loss continued throughout the day and by the middle of the night I was in bad shape. My parents told me later I was as "white as a sheet," and my Dad could find no pulse. My mom got into the car once more and headed for the hospital where she found a female doctor on duty who agreed to see if she could help me.

In the meantime, my dad was there by the couch with me, and I asked him, "Daddy, am I going to die?" His reply was, "No, you're not going to die." He knew God was probably the only one who could help me now, and he decided it was time to pray. He asked God to heal my body and stop the bleeding. It was a simple prayer, but one prayed from the heart. It was a big step of faith for my dad since he was a new Christian. By the time my mom returned with the doctor, the bleeding had stopped, and I had fallen asleep. By the next morning I was outside playing with my brother and sister. When my dad saw me, he sat down in total amazement. God had truly answered his prayer. Considering the amount of blood I lost during the past 24 hours there was no way I could be well enough to play outside.

Shortly after that incident, Emily began running a temperature of 104 degrees and went into convulsions. An ambulance was summoned, and she was taken to the hospital in Spokane. The doctors checked her over, diagnosed her with Nephritis, or Bright's Disease, and explained that the condition was fatal. There was another girl in Emily's room who was the same age and the same diagnosis who died of the disease. Emily remembers her being covered with a sheet and being taken from the room. My parents turned to God once more, and they asked the church congregation to join them in prayer. My parents were new in the faith, and they believed they could ask God to meet any need and He would meet it. He didn't disappoint them. Emily recovered, and God received the glory and praise!

Back in Massachusetts my parents stayed long enough to make sure I was feeling better, and then headed back to California. They left Emily with me; I always felt better when she was near. I made an appointment to see the doctor, and as soon as I explained that this was an "attack of the enemy," he said, "We'd better get you to a psychiatrist soon." He didn't understand I was talking about a spiritual enemy. Of course, the doctor prescribed a tranquilizer which made me feel better, but it continued to mask the problem and pain.

The next few weeks passed quickly, and we made the most of our time together. John invited Ben Casey over, and the four of us spent time together. We toured Boston, tried out new restaurants, and played Rook. Before I knew it, we were putting Emily on the plane to return to California.

John, me, my sister Emily, and John (Ben) Casey
1965

6

Assignment: Fort Wolters

Soon after Emily left, John received orders for his next assignment—Fort Wolters, Texas. We took out our trusty map and soon found it located in Mineral Wells, famous for the Crazy Water Hotel, and not too far from Fort Worth. We discovered Fort Wolters was the home of the Army's Primary Helicopter School. However, John would be assigned to the 303d Army Security Agency. We were offered a two-bedroom duplex on the post. Living in the connected duplex was a warrant officer's wife, Lisa Andrews, a woman from Germany with four small children. Lisa's husband was on assignment overseas.

After we settled in, I decided to make a quick trip to California to visit my family and planned to look for a job when I returned. My 14 year old brother, David, flew back to Texas with me. This was his first flight, and I remember him looking out the window while the plane was turning in a tight bank. His face turned white and in a nervous voice he exclaimed, "The plane has stopped in mid-air." As I looked out and down it did look like the airplane was suspended in air, but then the pilot finished the turn and we were leveled out again.

I was 11 years old when David was born and practically raised him. I remember feeding him, burping him, changing his diapers, and carrying him around on my hip. I watched over him like a mother hen. He stayed with us at Fort Wolters for a couple of months until it was time for him to return to school in California. He became a little homesick during the summer, so I'm sure he was ready to board the plane and head for home.

Soon after that, I obtained a job as a secretary in the Operations Office at the Primary Helicopter School. John and I furnished our duplex with furniture purchased from the Fingers Furniture Store in Fort Worth and were finally getting settled into a daily routine. We found a Baptist Church we liked in downtown Mineral Wells. The pastor's name was Don Turner, and we became friends with him and his family. I don't remember any of his sermons, but I do remember him quoting this Scripture from the Bible many times: "He that is not with me is against me; and he that gathereth not with me scattereth abroad," found in Matthew 12:30. That is the one Scripture that stuck in my mind, and I always think of Pastor Turner when I hear it.

Emily was working in a civil service job in California, and I remember telling her she should transfer to Fort Wolters. I was sure she would have no problem landing a job there, and, besides, there were lots of nice looking Army pilots and maybe she could find one she liked. She finally transferred to the Personnel Office on post and did eventually meet her future husband, Capt. Jim Barnes, from Rolla, Missouri.

By now it was Christmas 1965, and we decided to spend the holidays in Michigan with John's family. We packed up the car and headed north by way of Fort Worth. Somehow we took the wrong road out of Fort Worth, and John had to stop at a service station to get directions. John hated to travel with maps and baggage in the car, but he also hated to stop to ask for directions. Emily and I wanted maps in the car so we could help navigate, and so we had to chuckle a little when we became lost.

We spent Christmas at his sister Jackie's house. At that time, she and her husband, Mike, had three beautiful daughters, but they would finally have a son and a fourth daughter. All of John's nieces and nephews loved their "Uncle John," and he loved them in return. John's mom, Muriel, wrote a poem to honor her five children:

To My Children

The sweetest gift was brought to me
and five times over, too.
Each gift a jewel of priceless worth
God's gift to me was you.

A little girl so dark and cute
Was first to come my way.
Then very soon another miss
Was born at dawn of day.

We went along for several years
We four - of course, there's Dad!
We thought our family quite complete
And loved the gifts we had.

But then one day a darling girl
Was ours - We said, "Another?"
"What seems to be the trouble here
How do we get a brother?"

But he was just around the bend
And sister was still small
When brother came to join us
Much welcomed by us all.

Three sisters and a brother.
Folks said, "This is dandy."
But God had one more gift for me,
Along came wee Miss Sandy.

The house was full of noise and din
Mother's nerves were wearing thin.
"I'll be so glad when they are grown,"
She said - (to just herself alone).

But God said, "Wait, this must not be!
For I have given these gifts to thee
Each one a precious life to mold
To teach of Me - their souls you hold."

And you must guard these jewels so rare
That I have given you to share
For they are Mine and they must know
The One who gives - and loves them so."

And now today they've grown and gone
For years do pass, and time goes on
But deep within their hearts abide
The knowledge of their Christ who died.

Should they now wander from thy Way,
And from Thy path they go astray
I'd tell Thee, "Wait, this must not be
For I have given them back to Thee."

And You will guard these jewels so rare
That You and I for years did share
And lead them back once more to see
Thy Greatest Gift at Calvary.

John played the role of Santa Claus on Christmas morning and passed out all of the gifts from under the tree. There was so much excitement—wide-eyed children tearing open their packages and Christmas paper everywhere. The smell of coffee in the air, and breakfast cooking on the stove. Christmas Day is such a special time. It's even more special when you're with loved ones. It had so much meaning to us. It was far more than presents, trees, tinsel, Santa Claus, and the hustle and bustle of shopping. We were celebrating our Savior's birth, and we knew real life because of Him. If the world could only know the significance of this day.

Looking back, there would also be another significance to this Christmas; it would be John's last. He, too, loved Christmas: being with family, the beautiful carols, the real meaning of Christmas, and all the sights and sounds of the season. He spoke of happy childhood memories when he and his mom would stay up on Christmas Eve to listen to the Hallelujah Chorus. Soon enough, it was time to head back to Texas, and after many hugs, kisses, and good-byes, we were on our way down the road. We wouldn't forget this Christmas.

After the 1966 New Year's celebration, we returned to our work routine at Fort Wolters. John usually arrived home from work before I did and would spend time strumming his guitar and singing a few songs. When I arrived home, I'd usually find him still in his fatigues and combat boots stretched out on the couch fast asleep. I kissed him while he slept, unlaced his boots, and dropped them to the floor. I think he just pretended to be asleep because he liked me taking off those big boots.

John had a beautiful baritone voice and loved music. He traveled with the school choir when he attended Taylor University in Upland, Indiana. He was in charge of getting things set up before the concerts and then taking them down afterwards. Those days held fond memories for him.

John and his parents, Jack and Muriel Cochrane
Christmas 1965

7

Orders for Vietnam

Our country was in the middle of the Vietnam War, and, of course, rumors were always flying about whose unit would ship out next. I would mostly try to ignore the rumors and hope it would never be John's unit, but in my heart of hearts, I knew that sooner or later he would have to go. Isn't this what it was all about? John had extensive training for war. Besides graduating from OCS, he had recently completed the Airborne Training at Fort Benning, Georgia, and could now proudly wear the airborne wings on his chest. John also attended the Jungle Warfare School in Panama which included sleeping, eating, and living in the jungle. He even learned how to eat boa constrictors!

The day finally came when rumors became fact. The officers and men of the 303d ASA Battalion were going to Vietnam. There were so many things to complete and so many arrangements and decisions that had to be made that we barely had time to think, really think, about what the future might hold. One thing we knew for sure; John would be in hostile territory, and we'd be miles apart. We would have to once again depend on God and His protection and will to be done. He watched over us in the past, and we knew He could do it again.

The decision was made that I would return to California and stay with my parents while John was serving in Vietnam. He said if anything happened to him, he wanted me near my family, and I thought that was a good idea. Emily would remain in Mineral Wells, keep her job, and move in with a military wife whose husband was overseas.

John was approved for leave, so we headed to Michigan to tell his parents and family goodbye. It was very difficult. I remember John saying goodbye to his mom and dad outside their apartment in Westland. He never liked to see tears, but I remember lots of hugs and kisses. After all, we never expected he wouldn't be coming home. In one year he would be home again, and things would be back to normal.

When we got into our car to leave, John said he had a funny feeling about leaving his parents, as if he might not see them again. I quickly changed the subject and told him not to think like that. Everything would be fine, and he would be home again before he knew it. He had also told me in a previous conversation that if anything happened to him, he wanted to be buried at Arlington National Cemetery—"with all the war heroes," he added. And there was more. If anything happened to him, he wanted me to live life twice as full—for him, too. He said, "I want you to get married again if something happens to me." Did he really think something was going to happen to him, or did all of the soldiers going to war leave final instructions with their families just in case? I preferred to think the latter. I brushed these things from my mind and wouldn't allow myself to dwell on any negative thoughts regarding John. I prayed that he would come home again safe and sound.

It was April 1, 1966, when John and I headed for California in our 1965 Chevrolet Impala. He was taking me home, and he planned to fly back to Mineral Wells to accompany his troops on the train to the west coast before boarding a ship for Vietnam. John was like that. He wanted to be with his men on the train at such a difficult time—the first leg of the trip that would take them to a far away land to fight in a war no one understood.

We were together for a few short days, and then it was time for John to return to Texas. My brother Chuck and I took him to the Los Angeles Airport where he caught a flight to Fort Worth. I excused myself for a few minutes, and Chuck had a chance to talk to John in private. He told me later that he had asked John how he felt about the war and the possibility of losing his life in Vietnam, and he said John just shrugged his shoulders as if to say, "I'm in this now, and there's no turning back. Besides, God is the One in control." The return train ride would take the troops to San Francisco where they would board a ship, the USS Weigal, make a stop in San Diego Harbor, and then head out to sea. John called from San Francisco to let me know the day and time of their arrival in San Diego and where the ship would dock.

I contacted my girlfriend, Jan Norris, who lived in San Diego, and asked if she and her husband, Ted, would like to accompany me to the ship to see John off. Jan was with Emily and me when we met John in Japan three years earlier. Of course she said yes, so I made arrangements to stop by their house on the way to the ship. The USS Weigal was already docked when we drove up, and we were told by the officials that civilians would be able to board the ship to spend approximately one hour with their loved ones.

The gangplank was finally put into place, and we were allowed to go aboard. John was there to greet me. We went to an area with tables and benches and sat down with some of the other troops and their families. This was such a huge ship, and it looked like there were hundreds of men on board from every branch of the Service. Some conversations sounded light-hearted and carefree, while others were rather quiet. Everyone was lost in his or her own thoughts. I had a key ring with a furry aqua-colored ball at the end of it that smelled of perfume. I gave it to John and told him to keep it with his things. Every time he saw it or smelled the perfume he could think of me.

Since I was the only wife there from the battalion, I took requests from the soldiers in John's detachment. They asked me to order flowers for their wives or make telephone calls to girlfriends. I was glad I was there and able to carry out their wishes. The announcement to leave the ship came all too soon. John took my hand, pulled me up from the bench, and we stepped a few feet away from the crowd. He put his arms around me and squeezed tight, really tight, and planted a big firm kiss on my lips. Then he said, "I don't want any tears." A lump in my throat prevented me from speaking, even breathing was difficult. The tears were ready to roll down my cheeks, but I had to hold them back, at least until I got off the ship. I turned to walk down the gangplank to join Ted and Jan, and we stood on the dock for several minutes trying to locate John's face among the many other faces peering down from the huge ship. But then I found him. He was standing at the end of the row looking down at us with his handsome face. I asked Ted to snap a couple pictures of him, and the next thing I knew John was nodding his head for us to leave. He didn't want me to watch his ship depart; it would be too difficult, too final. The ship left San Diego Harbor on April 16, 1966, only three days before John's 25th birthday.

I returned to Jan and Ted's house before making the drive home to San Bernardino, and while I was there a dozen red roses were delivered with a card that simply read, "I love you - John." While I was taking the orders for the other men on board the ship, John had asked Ted to have flowers delivered to me at their house. How special and loved I felt! Now we just had to get through a one-year tour of duty in Vietnam before we would be together again. It couldn't come soon enough.

On the way home, I couldn't keep my mind on the driving. My thoughts were with John, and I couldn't concentrate. I was snapped back to reality when I saw a California Highway Patrolman behind me with his lights flashing. I quickly pulled over, and he pulled behind me. When he arrived at my car, he told me, in no uncertain terms, that I had been driving too fast, driving too close to the car in front of me, and changing lanes without using my turn indicator. Usually I am a safe driver. I explained that I was coming home from San Diego and had just seen my husband off on a ship to Vietnam. He offered his sympathy, but returned to his car and wrote out a ticket anyway.

I decided to appear in court several days later to see if the judge would have mercy on me. Well, once the charges were read, the judge asked if I had anything to say for myself. I explained my story again. The next thing I heard was the sound of the gavel and the words, "Case dismissed." "Thank you," I said with a sigh of relief.

8

Letters from Vietnam

My first letter from John after he left for Vietnam was dated the end of April 1966.

My Dearest Wife:

I have never been so bored in my whole life. I have walked this ship from one end to the other, read three long books, sat up on the sun deck until I look like the first cousin to a lobster, gained about six pounds, played a guitar until my fingers are numb and my voice hoarse, and to top it off, I have to almost knock myself out with exercise every night before I can fall asleep. I thought this shipboard living would agree with me, but I don't have a blasted thing to do from morning til night, and it is driving me nuts!

Tomorrow we are supposed to arrive in Okinawa after fifteen days at sea. Tomorrow is Saturday, that much I know. Our beloved colonel has put the word out that only officers and sergeants grade E-6 and above can get off the ship for only four hours at a time. Needless to say, this has the troops highly agitated almost to the point of mutiny. I spoke up and told him what I thought about his pass policy, and he blew up at me. I told him that the soldiers have been stacked up like animals in the hold and have either been working their tails off on detail aboard ship or are as bored as the rest of us from having nothing to do. I also mentioned that this would be the last chance for the men to walk around and take a free breath of air without having to worry about getting shot at or having a grenade blow them into a million pieces. Then, as if that wasn't enough, I told him that I didn't feel, as an officer, that

I could ask my men to fight hard if I hadn't been able to get them some time off in Okinawa. Besides, if these guys could be trusted to fight a war, then they could be trusted to go to town for a few hours.

Well, when I finished, my face was red as a beet, and I was shaking with indignation. I was all prepared to be decommissioned when Carroll Hughes and Dallas Scherk came up and stood beside me and told the colonel, "That goes for us, too, Sir."

The colonel then chewed us all out with rather colorful language and finally said, "You are all restricted to the ship when we get to Okinawa." But that's no big thing; there probably isn't much to do in Okie, anyway.

Well, I just returned from the colonel's cabin. He chewed us out about our conduct, but said that because we had been doing a good job in the past, he was going to overlook our "little discretion" this time and let us have liberty tomorrow. Not only that, but he's going to let everybody out on liberty for eight hours. So chalk one up for the lieutenants. Of course he also mentioned that he never wanted to hear that kind of talk out of a second lieutenant again. But that's not a problem. I make first lieutenant in another three months.

Well, Angel, let me tell you a little about this boat. We get up at 0700 and have breakfast; then we are free until 1130 hours when we eat again. Then comes the afternoon, which is also free time until 1630 when we have dinner. After dinner we are free until 2000 hours when we go to see a movie. Now, that's a subject close to my heart. You would not believe these movies.

Last night, for instance, we saw The Slave Ship, *starring Wallace Berry, and that sensational new discovery, Mickey Rooney. It was released in 1937 and was a great masterpiece of art only surpassed in excellence by the movie the night before,* Rose of Washington Square. *This great epic of the cinema was released in*

1939 and has been rejected by every television station in the States as being "too bad for our late-late-late show." It starred Tyrone Power before he was old enough to shave, and some silent movie star whose voice sounded like an out-of-tune piano, and the greatest of them all, Al Jolson. I mean these movies are the greatest. Last week we saw one called Trail Street, starring none other than Gaby Hayes. That one was too much, and I had to leave early.

However, if you don't want to go to the movies, there are several other things you can do. You can read, which I have done until my eyes are about ready to give out; play cards, which I have also done until my hands are crippled up from shuffling; and lastly, you can stand out on the deck and watch the moon, which I have also done until I thought I would break out crying because I was so lonesome for you. As a matter of fact, the most popular pastime aboard this old tub is crying—crying because we're separated from our loved ones, crying because we're here and because we're going where we don't want to, and just plain crying to cry. Of course the biggest problem is boredom—nothing to do so the days just drag by, piled one on top of the other, until you dread the thought of waking in the morning. I'm glad the colonel changed his mind about letting the troops off because if he hadn't, I do believe he would have had a riot on his hands.

Well, enough about me. How are things in sunny California? Is your dad feeling better yet? He is trying to do too much in too little time. And what about my mother-in-law? How is she getting along? You might pass the word on to them that I think about them all the time and still can't get over how beautiful the diamond ring is that they gave me for a birthday present. I've received several compliments and even a couple of offers to buy it. However, there isn't enough money on this tub to buy this ring. Thank them again for me, okay?

Tell Chuck thanks for going to the airport with us, and that I am sorry I didn't get to come up while we were in San Diego. Anyway, tell him I am about halfway through This Kind of War, *and I am really enjoying it. Also, tell him if he ever entertained any visions about taking a boat cruise, forget it. This isn't for him (or me for that matter).*

The guys threw a party for my birthday. It was a complete surprise! They had the ship's baker make a birthday cake and right after the movie we all came back to our cove; even the battalion officers were there. They had taken up a collection and bought me an instamatic camera, almost like the one you have, so I have been making like a camera bug. It's got a built-in flash attachment, flashbulbs, and the whole bit. A really nice camera and a real surprise. We sat around eating cake and drinking Cokes; I took some pictures of all of them. I will send the film to you, and you can have it developed.

The only other chance I had to use the camera was when we crossed the 180th Parallel Line. This is supposed to be a big thing aboard ship as it means you have crossed the International Date Line and lost a day. Anyway, the Marines aboard ship had an initiation for all the officers and men who had never been across the I.D.L. before. When you get the pictures, you will see men squirming around the deck after being dipped in a barrel of grease, proving that they are some kind of animals or something.

They just brought in the schedule for tonight's movie. It's The Haunting. *Sounds like a real winner. Well, m'love, how are you feeling? Has the doctor been able to help you yet? Does he think it's related to the tropical sprue? I sure hope it's not getting you down too much because I know how lousy it makes you feel. However, no matter what it is, get it taken care of. I have plans for us when I get back, and I want you well enough to enjoy them.*

Well, I just returned from the flick, and it was on the same line as Psycho. *It sure had me scared. I'd hate to see it alone.*

Tomorrow we reach "Okie." I am looking forward to getting off this tub and getting a nice Japanese bath. It seems funny to be back with the Japanese after all this time. It's almost like returning to meet old friends, even though I will be several hundred miles from where we were before. I am going to try to find a Kobe Steak House or a restaurant where I can get sukiyaki.

I understand I am going to be indisposed for your birthday. I will try to get you something in Okie. If not, then I will send it after I get to Vietnam. I don't even know what to get you, but I have a really good idea for Christmas. All I've got to do is find it.

Well, m'love, it's getting late, and I am going to hit the rack. Of course, I will probably have nightmares after that movie to-night, but, believe it or not, I am tired. I am serious about what I told you before. I don't care how long it takes or how much it costs, I want you better. If they have to put you in the hospital for a few days, it's okay with me. If you have to see a civilian doctor, just make sure you fill out the forms so the government will pay for it. The doctor will have the forms, I am sure. This sounds as if I am detaching myself from all feeling, but I am not. I am really wor-ried about you, Angel, especially these last few weeks. Don't let anything happen to you, doll, because you are the only thing I care about coming home to. Granted, sometimes I act as if I could care less, but I believe you know I couldn't stand this lousy world without you. Sometimes, and it's more often than you think, I can't stand myself or the rest of this crazy world. And then I look at you and I see how you are: honest, naive, and in some ways so inno-cent about things. And I think maybe man isn't so bad after all. And this helps me have new insights about things. This is pretty much a "mumble-jumble," but what I really mean is that you mean

*more to me than anything else on this earth. Take care of yourself,
darling; this young soldier needs you very much.*

*As you know, I had planned on writing you a day-by-day
account of this trip. Needless to say, it wouldn't have worked out,
as nothing special or exciting has happened. I may not write you
every day, lover, but you remember this: I think about you every
day and miss you more as each day goes by. You really grow on
me, Angel, almost like a second soul. I feel really close to you at
times like this, even though we are separated by 11,000 miles.
What it all boils down to, doll, is that I LOVE YOU VERY
MUCH.*

*I am going to say so long for now. I will send you a tape when
I get settled, plus letters in the meantime. Make a tape to send me.
I would truly love to hear your voice. Be good. Take care of your-
self and keep all your love for me.*

Much love,

J.

*P.S. The key chain has lost its smell. What kind of perfume
did you put on it anyway? Oh, yes—my address is: LT JFC, 17th
RRU, APO 96227, San Francisco, California.*

John sent my brother Chuck a letter dated 11 May 66, from Saigon, South Vietnam.

Greetings:

It's a balmy, warm night here in Saigon and if the heat doesn't keep you awake, the sound of the artillery batteries shooting "feeler" rounds will. They say that after awhile you get used to hearing the sounds of war, but I don't think I ever will.

I am sitting here on a dock along the Saigon River. I just finished a letter to Elaine and one earlier to my mother. Three letters in one day is almost a record for me. However, there is so little free time here, and one learns to take advantage of a lull and catch up on unfinished things. As I sit here writing under the spotlights that illuminate the pier, my eye keeps getting distracted by darting shadows both on the ground and in the air. Closer observation shows the shadows to be rats. I don't believe I have ever seen so many, and big ones, too. I'd be lying if I said they didn't make me just a bit nervous. In the air the shadows are bats, not like the ones on the "Batman Show," but smaller like a canary or sparrow. They are almost too numerous to count and fill the air with their high pitched shrieks. I can't say bats are some of my best friends, either. It's times like this I want to pinch myself to see if I am dreaming, or say to myself, "What am I doing here?"

Well, enough of the morbid aspects of this country. In peace time I think I would like Saigon. It is a large city, built along the same lines as Paris. Sidewalk cafes are on almost all streets. The streets themselves, contrary to most of the Orient (except Tokyo), are wide and have boulevards down the middle with trees and benches for the people to enjoy. The traffic is terrible which is why they have nice parks and boulevards. Once you get off the grass and onto the pavement, it's every man for himself. I would not say it's worse than Tokyo, but if any of the Kamikaze's left Japan after

*the war, then they're probably driving cabs. Chuck, you would
appreciate the situation. Imagine yourself and two others your size
crammed into a tiny Renault cab, driving around sixty miles per
hour down the San Bernardino Freeway at about 5:30 p.m. heading east in the west bound lane. That's what I feel when I get into
one of these cabs.*

*The architecture in the more exclusive sections of town is strictly
French Provincial with most of the houses having large stone walls
around them. Of course, the war has changed the city a lot. The
curfew is midnight, and after that the city is like a morgue. The
only ones remaining on the street are the homeless, of which there
are many, and the M.P.s. The night before last an M.P. column
was ambushed in downtown Saigon as they were coming back
from changing guard by a group of Cong in an open truck. The
M.P.s wiped them out. This is the second time it's happened, but
last time the Cong killed several of the M.P.s. Now the score is
even, except for the dead. Things will never be even for them. The
same night we went out to dinner about a mile from where the
ambush took place. The restaurant was recommended to us by
one of my classmates at OCS. It is a small little "hole in the wall,"
nice looking but not by any means plush. However, I think I had
a meal that would be pretty hard to beat. I had Chateaubriand
steak, with french fries, a large tossed salad, expresso coffee and
the biggest, most delicious bowl of French onion soup I have ever
had—all for little more than 300 piaster (118 piasters to a dol-
lar). I sat there and ate until I couldn't move. Just thinking about
that soup makes me want to throw these C Rations in the river. It
was terrific.*

*I don't think I ever mentioned why I am down here at the
river. We unloaded quite a bit of gear today, and some of it is
classified; thus, they need a guard detail. I am it! Or rather five of
my men are guarding. I am guarding them.*

Last Sunday we all went up to Bien Hoa which will be our permanent camp if we ever get all our gear in. The place where we are slated to set up is a flat open field without grass or any trees around. When it rains, it's a pool of mud. When it's dry, you choke on the dust. In general, I would say it's a typical place for an Army camp. We figure it will take about two months before we can start to work, so the next few months should be quite hectic. However, like everyone else, I am anxious to get going. The days on the boat and the days here waiting for the equipment have me about bored to death. It will feel good getting back to work.

Well, I see it's almost time for the shift to change so I had better go post the new guard. I just wanted you to know I was glad to hear from you, and, last but not least, to thank you for watching out for Elaine for me. She listens to you and values your opinion, so I would ask you to make sure she continues to go to Narramore's Counseling Center until she is finally and completely over this thing. She has a tendency to get discouraged when she doesn't see results, so see to it that she keeps going. I would appreciate it; she means an awful lot to me.

Well, y'all, I see my sergeant's getting a little impatient, so I guess I had better go hold his hand. Kiss the kids for me and remember me in your prayers as I do you.

God bless y'all
J.

And then I received a letter written on my 26th birthday, May 18, 1966 as follows:

My Dearest Wife:

Much love to you on your 26th. I am sorry we couldn't be together for it. If I were there, we could go out for dinner, maybe take in a play or a show, then come home to our oversized "adult playpen" and cap off a beautiful night.

Since I last wrote you I have moved from beautiful, big Saigon to dirty little Bien Hoa. Actually the area is Long Binh, but it's still dirty and little. Our equipment still hasn't arrived, at least not all of it. So we are virtually stuck here in the muddy water with no way to get out. The area I described in my last letter is where we are now. The mud on rainy days (and every day is a rainy day) is up to the ankles, and everybody is living in tents. Right now I am sitting on a wooden box in my tent (which I share with Carroll Hughes who is gone to Da Nang for two weeks) in my green Army shorts, with nothing else on but my shower shoes and my wrist-watch, and I am just dripping sweat. There is little or no breeze in this area even though I have the sides of the tent up. The mosquitoes are buzzing around like jet fighters. They circle overhead until they see an opening and then they dive. Sometimes I get them, but most of the time I miss. Consequently I look a lot like a golf ball with lumps all over me.

You will never guess what I am using for a light — an old pre-Revolutionary War model of a kerosene lantern. It's made of glass and has a regular wick set up with a glass globe. It's a real winner. It cost me 50 piaster at a local junk store.

As I was writing this last line I heard a tremendous explosion. I looked outside just in time to see two big jet fighters drop napalm on a jungle area about a mile from where we are. The light from the fire is just about bright enough to write by. I can still hear gunfire, so I guess they haven't got all of 'em yet. Boy, that fire is really making it hot. As I got up to look, I could see the imprint of my wet little bottom on the plywood box. I mean, it is really hot over here. During the day the temperature usually is 100 degrees, and the humidity is about 99 per cent, so it is miserable. About the only time it's really nice is early morning, about five or six a.m. But then, by 8:30 or 9 a.m., I am soaked through.

I don't know what's happening over to the south of us, but for the last forty five minutes or so I have been standing with John Walker and the colonel, watching a blaze over there. There are all kinds of small arms fire and artillery. Sounds like a real pitched battle. I hope they leave us alone.

You know, Darling, it's rather weird over here. I'm writing you a letter in comparative safety, not giving much thought to the fact that there is a war going on. We are mainly concerned with our own creature comforts such as getting wood to put over our muddy floors and building showers to use. And yet, not more than a mile from where I sit, untold numbers of human beings are being killed. Not just Americans, but Australians, Koreans, Vietnamese and Viet Cong. This really makes me stop and think. It is very possible, and quite probable, that I will spend my whole year here without ever having seen a V.C., yet they are all around us as can be evidenced by the shooting.

During the day I could almost swear that there is no war here. In Saigon, with the exception of the guards and barbed wire, you would never suspect there was a war. Yet, when the night comes, the fires from the bombs and the shooting from both sides wipes out any question regarding the validity of this war.

I will say one thing from what I have seen here. Even with all its fault, and there are many, we have the greatest Army in the world, and without a doubt, the finest soldiers. I am proud to be one of them. I feel sorry for the V.C., or for any enemy that enter-

tains thoughts of beating us in war. We may get bogged down in our political squabbles and lose face and ground by doing nothing because of our lousy politicians, but when the last card is played and the last speech said and the armies clash in battle, ours can't be beat. If you could see the vast amounts of equipment and resources and manpower we have, you would better understand what I mean.

Well, enough of that.

It is now 10:20 p.m. here or 2220 hours Army time; so that would make it about 5 a.m. or 0520 on the 18th where you are. You are probably asleep right now; at least, you'd better be. You've probably got on your white nightgown, the one you wore in Japan that first night, and oblivious to the world around you right now. Total innocence in sleep. I can only improve on the picture by changing it so that I am there with you, and you are asleep in my arms. I miss you very much as I do every night, but maybe if it's possible, even more so tonight because of what I have seen and because it's your birthday. I have nothing for your birthday yet, because I have found nothing that quite measures up to what I am looking for. I will get you something, but when I do it will be something that can convey my love to you as I feel it now. It may be that I will have to wait until I can get enough money. But you will get something.

The colonel just stopped by again and reminded me that tomorrow is Ho Chi Minh's birthday, and that we are all restricted to the area for the day. This doesn't really mean much, seeing as how I have been stuck here for almost a week anyway. It seems that the G-2 thinks the local V.C. have something planned to give old Ho Chi a good present. I wish them luck; they will probably need it.

Well, lover, it's late, and I am going to close for now. I doubt whether I will sleep much with all the noise around here, but at least I am going to try. Remember that I love you very much, and that I need you there waiting for me and loving me. I pray daily for your deliverance from your illness and trust the Lord to bring me safely home to a wife in good health. Tell your folks to keep those letters coming, and that I will write them when I get a chance. Give my love to all at home, both in California and Michigan. But most of all, to my best girl who's having a birthday today.

Again, I love you, Angel, and am dreaming of the day you will once more be in my arms and the separation will be behind us. Write when you can.

Love,

J.

Back home in California, I was settling into a routine and living at home with my parents until John returned from Vietnam. Since I was still feeling depressed, I was referred to the Narramore Christian Center in Pasadena for counseling. I was scheduled for two appointments each week and would drive through heavy traffic, which took over an hour each way. I went for several weeks, but was not really feeling any benefit from the private counseling sessions. Since I was a Christian, I remember asking the counselor if what I was going through was the work of Satan—all the fears and feelings of hopelessness, guilt, and doubts. It was like I was caught in quicksand and couldn't get free. The more I tried to get free, the worse it got. And it wasn't like I could "just snap out of it," or "think positive;" nothing seemed to help. I was caught in a black hole of despair and couldn't climb out. The counselor didn't have any real solid answers for me. He said the possibility was there, but he didn't seem to know how to help me. I continued taking tranquilizers, but I knew that wasn't the answer. It was like putting a Band-aid on a deep festering wound. It wouldn't bring healing, but only temporary relief.

I loved getting letters from John. It was the bright spot of my life. I loved the way his letters described situations and circumstances in such a way that I felt like I was right there with him.

I'm sorry to say that some of John's letters, or portions of his letters, were unfortunately destroyed when I lived in Colorado in the early 1970s. I became friends with a girl whose husband was Missing in Action (MIA) in Vietnam, and she said she had destroyed all of her husband's letters because she knew if she kept them, she would spend her time living in those letters. She influenced me, and thus the next letter and other letters I will share, are missing some pages.

I received a letter dated 29 May 1966, 1232 hours:

My Dearest Wife:

Today is Sunday, and you'd never know it. I haven't been to church today. Maybe I can make it tonight.

Things have really taken a turn for the worse around here. Everybody is mad at everybody else. The staff has been directing the Company, and the officers have been treated like kids. It's getting to the point where a lieutenant is little better than good for nothing.

The problem is this: We have an operations area to build so that we can do our job. But along with that, there are also the troops to think of. They have been here a month and are still living like pigs in mud. The lieutenants have dragged their feet on the operations end of things in order to give our troops time to build up the living area.

Well, lover, I must check on my platoon now, so I will close. Tell your mother that those verses she sent (Psalms 9:9 and 10) arrived at a good time because I was feeling a bit oppressed at the time myself. I have been reading my Bible quite a bit over here; not as much as I should perhaps, but much more than I have in the past. I remember each of you in prayer daily and trust you do the same for me. I especially pray that the Lord will be nearer to you during these months while we are apart. And, of course, that He will heal you of your sickness. Without Him to turn to, I don't know what I would do.

I love you, Angel, and sometimes don't believe I will be able to make it without you by my side. The days are going by fast—faster than I had hoped. It won't be long, perhaps faster than you think.

The following letter was dated 28 June 1966, 2100 hours:

My Dearest Wife:

Greetings on a wet, muddy, murky night. I am still at Bien Hoa but am due to leave pretty soon. I should be out of here around the first of July and at my next station by the fourth. Who knows, maybe I will even get the fourth off.

I am feeling much better again. I still have the hacking cough, but I feel good at least. I have used up all the cough syrup and pills you sent, so I guess they helped.

My last letter was pretty bad. I should have never written when I did. I was sick, tired and mad about several small things. Needless to say, this doesn't make for the best attitude in which to write to one I love. Tonight, however, I feel a lot better but am still tired and still mad a little, and I still love you a lot.

I have been thinking a lot about my forthcoming move. The area in which I am going is Lai Khe in Bien Long province. I will have a platoon much like the detachment I had in south Texas. I will be the only officer from our outfit. The others will be Infantry or Artillery. Needless to say, I will be away from the bedlam and panic of this battalion, and believe me, Angel, that's good. Lai Khe will be our base camp, but we will be traveling with the 1st Division when they go on missions. It is what I feel I should be doing. I am just not made for garrison duty. I need to be on the move, not just sitting behind a desk. Not that the job I have now is like that, because it isn't yet. But we are almost finished, and soon it will be a desk job. And I don't like that one bit. Carroll is a bit jealous of me; at least, he tells me he is. Of course, while this area isn't the greatest in the world, it's better than where I will be. We will be moving a lot, and I suppose I will be sleeping on the ground for awhile. I must be crazy, but I am looking forward to it. At least I will feel as if I am really helping in this stupid war.

I understand I will have about 40 men under my control. I will have help in the form of a platoon sergeant, but I will be responsible for everyone. I'm glad I am not expected to send these men into battle. I don't even know them, but I wouldn't like the choice of who lives and who dies. I don't think I am a big enough man to do something like that. I would feel as if I were taking God's job away from Him. He is the only Person who decides who lives and who dies. I'll tell you one thing—He has been closer to me these past few weeks than ever before. I stop to think how one stray shot could kill me, and then I get to thinking. Were it not for the grace of God, I could have been knocked off several times already. He's been good to us, keeping me safe. How does one go about thanking God?

I got old Henry Greenfarb in the mail the other day along with the candy. Tell Margie I love her. She's the greatest poet I ever met. I really got a kick out of the poem. Old Henry sits on my desk and every time I see him, I have to chuckle. He's something else. The candy lasted exactly one and a half days, but it was enjoyed.

Hi John:
My name is Henry Greenfarb,
I've been sent across the sea.
I may not be too handsome,
But I hope that you like me.

Elaine was shopping in the store,
And spied me on display.
She handled me and made a face,
And almost walked away.

Then she thought of someone far,
A special guy she knew.
So she wrapped me up and mailed me off,
Now, here I am with you.

I may not be much company,
I know I'm not too cute.
I cannot walk and cannot talk,
And never will salute.

Now I'm in the Army,
I guess I'm on your staff.
So I'll always try to smile,
And give your men a laugh.

Who knows how useful I may be,
I may help win this war.
If I scare the enemy,
Just write Elaine for more.

Your Friend,
Henry Greenfarb

(Written by Margie—Elaine's younger sister)

Don't worry, Angel. The day will never come that I am untrue to you. I am a man, not an animal. And whereas sometimes the desire gets so big I feel I cannot contain it, I will because that is what sets man and animal apart. Besides, lover, I don't really have a choice. After we were married and I really learned what love was, I knew without a doubt I could never do anything to tarnish that love. Let's face it, I am hooked. It may be miserable while I am here and you are there, but believe me, Angel, the minute I hold you in my arms again, all this will be forgotten, and it will be like this separation never took place.

About this move, I think I told you I am going to Lai Khe, a little town about 100 kilometers north of here. It is with the 1st Infantry Division. Though it's true I will be in the field with the Infantry, I will still be doing the same type of job. I am not going to be up front shooting bullets and getting shot at. I am still in ASA and am in support of these people. I will be behind the front lines and as safe as if I were home in California on the freeway at rush hour. Don't worry about me. Just trust the Lord to watch over me and bring me home safely. I have complete trust in His will in my life. If it does happen that I get into battle up there, I have complete faith that the Lord's Will will be done. To worry about things like that is a waste of our time. As you said, "We cannot limit God." He is much wiser about running our lives than we could ever be. We can see in our own lives where He has led us from the very day we met. How can we think that He let all this happen just to have it end over here in this lousy jungle. I really believe that there is a purpose behind all this. I don't know what it is yet, but I know beyond a shadow of a doubt that there is a reason for it. We may know someday why, maybe not. In any case, I have quit worrying about it. I'll come home to you, lover. Never doubt that.

I got a letter from your mom which included a few lines from your dad. Tell your dad for me that I have learned quite a lot about constructing buildings and things like that. If he ever decides he needs a foxhole or a machine gun bunker on the property, don't worry. He's got the best foxhole digger and machine gun bunker-builder in the whole world right in his own family. You can also tell him that after next April 15th, he can count on having an extra two hands around to help him whenever he needs it. I may not be as big in stature as the Foster boys, but I'll bet I work cheaper. All I ask is a little loving in return from his oldest married daughter.

I also got a letter from my sister, Sandy. She is a really proud mother. All she talks about is "Robbie this" and "Robbie that." You'd think that she was the only one of the Cochrane girls ever to have a kid. She isn't, you know, because she said in the last line of her letter that Jackie just had her baby—a boy. She didn't say another word about it except that the Marriotts are all deliriously happy. Just think, all those beautiful little girls and now a boy. Some people have all the luck!

Well, lover, only two more things. The first is that I made first lieutenant today, which should increase the coins next month. I haven't been officially notified by the colonel yet, but I saw the message on it today, so I guess I can start wearing the silver bar. That's kind of funny because I don't even have one yet. However, those coins will come in handy. We are going to need a good bank account when I get out or I may not be able to afford to quit. The phrase for this family until I get the degree is "Save the coins, lover." It may be a long, hot summer next year.

The second thing I wanted to say is I love you very much. I continually thank the Lord for directing my life and leading me to you. I wish there were some other way to express my love for you than by just writing it out on paper. Words do not express how I feel or any gift or other gesture I could make. There is just no way to show you how much, not yet, anyway. So I will say it once again.

I love you, Angel.

J.

In July, I went back to work at Aerospace. I decided I needed to save some money for our R & R (Rest and Recuperation) trip to Hawaii which would be coming up in about three months. It couldn't come too soon for me.

Here's another letter John wrote to my brother Chuck and his family, dated 21 July 1966, 1415 hours:

Dear Chuck, Ruby, Debbie, and "Tiger":

How goes everything back in the promise land? I was cleaning out my desk today; it's the monthly cleaning where I take all the junk I hoard for a month and throw it into "file 13," when I came across a letter I had written to you quite some time ago. As a matter of fact, it was written the night of the Big Alert; the night we all sat around in the mud and rain waiting for "Charley" to attack. Needless to say, Charley had too much brains to come out in that mess, so all we accomplished was the loss of a night's sleep and a lot of rusty weapons. Anyway, afterwards I couldn't get to sleep so I wrote you a letter.

I have enjoyed hearing from you whenever you've had the chance to write. However, I am perhaps the world's most lousy letter writer. I even hate to sit down and write my folks. It just seems like a waste to me because half the time I can't really get across what I want to say anyway. Unfortunately, it wasn't something they taught me at OCS.

Two hundred and sixty-nine (269)—remember that. That is exactly the number of days I have to go before I can join the ranks of civilian. I don't really know what I'm going to do. I will go back to school, I know that. I suppose I will go on in Psychology, but, believe it or not, I really don't know yet what I want to do. Maybe some day, when I grow up, I will be able to sit down and figure my life out, but as of this time, I will just hang loose and play the breaks the way they fall. Actually, that's not true. I have prayed a lot about what to do, and I have every confidence that the Lord is going to show me what it will be. He just hasn't decided to let me know yet. Who knows? Maybe if I knew what it was, I wouldn't like it, and I'd decide to stay in the Army. I think what He wants me to do is commit myself. Then He will open the doors.

In any case, what I would like to do would be to get into some kind of work with kids, either juveniles or parolees, or something like that. I was impressed with your ideas because they run right along the same lines I have been thinking. You know, I really think we could do a good job in that area. I think we could both communicate with kids in their own way and with the emphasis on Christian living and Christ Himself. We would really have a product I would be proud to sell, and something kids could really use. It's a great idea. The how, where, when, or why is still in the dream stage, but I'll bet if we could find an angle, we could do it. It would really be something to work for.

I will be taking advantage of Uncle Sam's GI Bill for a couple of years—probably at UCR or maybe even your old alma mater; I don't really know. It's been so long since I have done any serious studying I don't even know if I can do it anymore. One thing I will say, however, is after being here for a year, I think I will be ready to give the "cottage & white picket fence" routine a chance, at least for awhile. I suppose when all my credits are figured out I will have about two more years to go for a BA or BS. So by the time I get the degree, I will probably have to limp across the stage using a seeing-eye dog or a cane to get it. However, at least I will be home which is where I belong. That, in itself, is enough to make me work to get what I want.

Well, I will close for now. I have a meeting to attend and if the Captain didn't have a chance to chew me out for something or other it would probably ruin his whole day.

Be good, take care, and give the kids a big kiss from "Uncle John." If you have any extra, you might also plant one on my beautiful wife for me—just to keep her in practice. Remember me in your prayers as I do you all.

J.

Another letter from John dated, 11 September 1966, 1730 hours:

Dear Angel,

Just a short note—primarily to send you a picture that Hobart Bentley took of Carroll Hughes and me with his Polaroid. I want to send it now because I leave for Daria tomorrow at 1330 hours and will not have a chance to write for a couple of days.

There is nothing more to tell you about anything. No news about Hawaii or anything else.

You can see Carroll has a pretty good handlebar mustache in this picture. To be truthful, mine looked bad. I couldn't keep from messing with it; consequently, I shaved it off about the first week of August. He was hugging himself in the picture, so he messed up the thing. He made some off the wall comment about how good looking he was; thus, I laughed and the gap shows. So it's not a good picture of either of us. But Bentley was out of film, so it's the best I could do.

Nothing else to report except I have received all your mother's letters and I apologize for not writing her. I have been meaning to, but I figure you pass on any news to her anyway, so I guess she knows what happens. Tell her I enjoy her letters very much and that she is the sweetest, kindest mother-in-law I have ever had, and I love her dearly.

While I am passing out all this love, the biggest share goes to you. A whole bunch as a matter of fact. Be good and see you soon.

Much Love,

J.

I received this letter from John, dated 21 September 1966, 1600 hours, Binh Hoa, Vietnam:

My Dearest Wife:

I am back here at battalion between assignments. I finished up with the Australians yesterday morning and got back here late last night. You might be interested in what is happening here although just thinking about it ticks me off!

While I was gone this last time, for just a week, a new lieutenant came into the unit. He had little experience in what I am doing, about one third as much as I have. So the colonel, being the great, omnipotent leader he is, decided that this was the time to further old John Cochrane's career. So he moved this new lieutenant into my slot, and he moved me into the XO[Executive Officer] slot of a new unit coming into the country. Now, if I were interested in staying in the Army, this would be great because it's an altogether new concept being employed and should bring glory on those connected with it. So he moved me out of a set-up, a plush set-up that I busted my back to get done so that I could enjoy it. Now I have a new unit that I have to break in. This means that I now have to live out in the mud, build new tent floors, new operations centers, etc. Plus the fact that my new commander is brand new with no experience. The other lieutenant there is the same way, and I don't have half the experience I should have to do the job.

Sometimes I wonder what they expect me to do. I can't create miracles. And because I was lucky here and did the job in record time, they are going to expect the same thing again. April can't get here soon enough for me.

I picked up my mail yesterday and along with a letter I also received your Airogram from the MARS station there at Norton

AFB. *It was great, and I really appreciated it. To answer your question—No, I have not received any of the packages you sent including the honey and nut bread although I would love to have it now.*

I received the pictures of you in the jeep, and the one that makes you look like a member of "Hell's Angels." You don't quite make a motorcycle "moll."

Carroll Hughes has been to Hong Kong and back. He picked me up a Rolex watch. It's not exactly what I wanted, but it's good enough. I also picked up a few assorted things for you. It is by no means what I would have liked to get you, but at least it's a token.

I haven't heard any more about R&R to Hawaii although I have been told I would get the next allocation. Major Smith just got back today. It should be around the middle of October before we go. I think I will just go ahead and send you the date of my arrival and you can meet me there. If not, then a lot of time is going to be wasted calling you after I get there, etc. If I don't make the flight, then I would still have a chance of calling you. Plus, if nothing else, you could stay with your friends there until I arrive.

I suppose Mom and Dad are back home by now. I bet they had a real ball. I had one card from them all the time they were in London. I'll be glad to see them again, if I ever get home.

This isn't much of a letter, but it has been almost a week since I have written, so I wanted to get something to you. Fred Budzyna just came in and gave me a package.

Larry, Chip, Carroll, and I are sitting here discussing my plight. Everyone is in agreement; I got taken. However, the colonel has made the decision, and we lowly lieutenants have nothing to do but to do his bidding, unquestioning as "lambs led to the slaughter."

Well, lover, I must bid you a good night. To say I love you is to risk wearing out a much used phrase. Except in this case you know I really mean it. I started this letter early this afternoon. It's now late, about eleven o'clock. Don't worry too much about my complaining and my new job. I am ticked off about it, but it's no big deal. I will survive. April will come, I will be home again with you, and all this nonsense will be nothing but a memory. And I will have nothing but miserable memories and crazy stories to tell to one and all. The only thing that is constant around here, no matter what job I am working or where I am staying, is that I love you and miss you very much. Hawaii may be only for five days, but with you there it will be a like a lifetime. I will write you again soon. Until then, be good, take care, and keep loving me.

    AML,

    J.

John in Vietnam. He wrote on the back of the photo,
"The Lone Lieutenant and His 'Horse', 18 August 1966"

25 September 1966, 1530 hours, Binh Hoa, Vietnam

My Dearest Wife:

We have just had our first death. Captain James D. Stallings was killed by a command-detonated mine at 1500 hours this afternoon.

He was returning from a mission and completely protected by flak vest, steel pot, and all the rest. "Charley" picked his vehicle to blow up and the four people were all seriously injured. But he was killed. The mine blew the whole vehicle apart, and the rest were very lucky.

It just goes to show that no matter what protections you take, no matter what precautions you use, when the Lord picks out your time, you go.

It would be nice if you dropped Ann a line. He had four kids.

One of my troops was driving the vehicle. I have to go and see how he is. He is right up the street in the 73d Medical Evacuation Hospital.

The whole battalion now will feel the effect of this war. We have been lucky so far—five months in the country with no serious casualties. This is the first, but I am afraid not the last.

Will write more later.

J

I can't help feeling that there must be something—some reason for it. Maybe it's a warning to the rest of us; if nothing else, it's a warning to me. "Life is like a vapor." Nothing is sure or constant. Yesterday Captain Stallings was a living, breathing man with a wife and four kids. Today he has been reduced to a paper bag of valuables, and his wife is a widow with four kids. If there is any comfort in it, it is that she will never want for anything. The government pays for the kids' education plus the $10,000 insur-

*ance and other benefits will keep her financially secure. So all she
has lost is her husband. How do you put a price tag on that?*

*And now what about him? Is he in heaven tonight or hell?
His dogtags say he was Baptist. So I assume he knew The Way.
Whether he followed it is a question only God can answer. How
about the rest of us here? If it were one of the others, where would
we be? Thank goodness I know that if it were me, then the Lord
would welcome me. Maybe not with open arms, but I would be
with Him. This is the tragedy in my life. If my life were put on a
scale, it would be terribly misbalanced. I have not done my share
in serving Him.*

*I received a poem in the mail today from the church. It's
called "Wasted Time," and I marvel at the fact it arrived today. It
sums up just what I have been talking about.*

When you think of all the effort
That is wasted every day
And the time we spend on pleasure
On the games we like to play.

Nothing wrong in being happy
Or enjoying what we do
Yet it won't have too much value
When this mortal life is through.

All the trophies and the prizes
And the medals we have won
All they'll be is dust collectors
When our life down here is done.

All the time we've spent in pleasure
And just building up our name
Won't be worth a worn-out penny
When we're no more in this game.

Life! Now there's a game worth trying
It's the greatest game on earth
If you really think you've got it
Here's the place to prove your worth.

Serving God and living daily
With your eyes on heaven's shore,
Storing up your future treasures
Where there's pleasure evermore.

You will not become as famous
When you live your life this way.
And you may not be invited
To the functions of the day.

Yet, your time will not be wasted
Or your effort been in vain,
When you spend them for the Master
And not just on selfish gain.

The poem about sums it up. Why do I find it so hard to live that way? I know in my head that it is the only way a Christian can live, yet I still hold back in certain areas. Why? What must I do to make me change? Why can God be so real to me, closer than I can ever explain, yet I still know there are areas He wants me to change. But I don't. Why does He put up with me? Surely there must be a limit even to His love and patience.

Well, I didn't intend to get wrapped up in this; at least not to this extent. It's just that I think these thoughts, and when I sit down to write you, it just pours out. Not a very good letter, I know. But it is the only outlet I have. I hope you don't get bored with it all. If I couldn't tell you my thoughts, I guess I would really be in bad shape.

I have to push so that I can leave tomorrow. I love you very much, Angel. You do know that, I think. You cannot know how much you are in my thoughts these days. It's almost as if you were an extension of my own body. I really miss you and even though I know I wouldn't have been happy not coming over here, I hope for and constantly pray that the Lord may let me return to you once again when my tour is up here. Until then, I give you all my love once again.

J.

5 October 1966, 1930 hours, Long Binh, Vietnam

My Dearest Wife:

My morale was low; I felt like quitting because the world was against me and it wasn't worth it anyway. Then the mailman came. I had two letters from you plus a package. The package was the photos, and, Darling, they are great. I especially like the close-up of you sitting on the back of the truck. You look good enough to eat. In fact, all the pictures make you look great. Tanned, healthy, and seemingly overflowing with an inner glow. You look like a million bucks—two million bucks!

I also received the two Paul Harvey columns along with the other article. I enjoy reading his column. He surely doesn't beat around the bush about Christianity! He believes it and doesn't hesitate a bit to write a column about it.

I also received your sermon. It was a comfort because I am fighting a battle within myself here. There is a lot of temptation here just to forget all about Christ and Christianity. People here are away from their families, and their lives and language drop to the lowest. Sometimes it's kind of hard not to pick up mannerisms of speech from those around you.

I remember telling you once up at Fort Devens, after I shot my mouth off about a card game, that when you work in and around filth all day long, some of it rubs off on you. Well, I have come pretty close to it a few times these last few weeks. Captain Stallings' death made me realize the trap I was beginning to fall into, though not intentionally. I was beginning to see no reason in trying to fight something bigger than I was. I had momentarily forgotten that it wasn't bigger than Christ. He's in charge, as He has been. Just a bit of old J.F.C. trying to push his weight around.

So it was quite a blow to me when Stallings got it. I got to thinking that there isn't any of us that far from instant eternity. But

as I Corinthians 10:13 says, He can handle it. I don't mean by
this that I am any more of a saint than I was when I left. But I can
tell you this. I have learned to have complete faith in God's plan
for me, and I am trying my best to live for Him each day.

I haven't quit smoking yet, and I wish I could. But like that
article you sent me said, I am hooked. I know God can take it
away, but I am holding back, the same as you when you were
depressed. You knew that all you had to do was ask Him to take
charge of it, and He would.

Well, that's the same problem I have. I ask Him to take away
the desire, yet the first time I feel myself getting pressured about
something, I grab for a smoke. I even quit carrying a lighter and
cigarettes. But people are only too happy to give you both. I even
told my platoon that I was quitting, and if I asked for a smoke,
don't give me one. All I did was get more nervous and nervous until
I actually had to go to one of my men and ask for one. He gave it
to me. I guess I am gutless.

You asked me about my new unit. Well, as I told you, it's the
11th Armored Cavalry. A modern day F Troop with tanks and
armored personnel carriers instead of horses. My work is classified, of course. But we support the regimental commander. There
are seventy seven enlisted men and three officers in the outfit, and
I am the operations officer, which means I handle all the operational aspects of the job (that figures, doesn't it?). Not quite as
glamorous as my last job, but much more demanding. Before, I
ran the show for myself and my fifty men. Now I have to plan
things for the others according to what my commanding officer
and the "Full Bull" ahead of the regiment want. I am required to
know about forty times as much as before, and you know me; I
learn slowly. It's not really a bad job. I guess I just didn't want to
leave my platoon or the few friends I had at battalion.

Right now we are in what is called a staging area—an area about a mile from battalion just east of Bien Hoa, and we will stay here until we get all our equipment in and get our permanent area cleared of Viet Cong so that we can set up a permanent base camp. Of course we will be on the move a lot, but the base camp is where we will call home. We should be moving into the permanent site around December sometime. Until then I have the job of getting all the equipment operational and the troops (seventy five per cent of whom just came out of school) trained. It keeps me plenty busy, and, of course, Captain Gentry and Ted, the other lieutenant, have their jobs to do, also. If we do the job right, we will be "writing the book" as far as operations of this sort are concerned. It hasn't ever been done before. We're learning.

Last Sunday we took our eight tracks (APC's) out and fired the fifty caliber machine guns and M-60 machine guns at a range near here. It was the first time most of the troops (including the commanding officer) had ever fired one. Of course I hadn't fired one since OCS, but still I knew enough to teach them. It was good training. It seems like an awful waste to me, though. The government spends all this money to train these 77 men and buys all the equipment. It's expensive ($130,000 per track), and we have eight of them. Each track is loaded with equipment, and it took the government-employed civilians six months to install the equipment. When they left the States, the college-trained engineers who draw about $50,000 per year to install this stuff, took it all out and had it packed. Now I have to get $150 per month PFC's who have never even seen the equipment before, to reinstall and operate it. Sometimes Old Sam doesn't use his head.

Time goes by fast. That's one good thing, at least.

I am still young and am not afraid to work. Besides, I want to see you, hold you and love you again, and I want to do it now, not six months from now.

You might drop a line to Dad and see if there is anything he can do for us such as reservations or anything else like that. What I would love to do when we get there is rent a car and travel over the island. You have some friends there, right? Maybe we could drop in on them, also. This will be almost like a honeymoon for us. We'll be all alone with nothing to do. It's only four days, but four days beats the heck out of anything we have had for the past five months. I want to stay in a hotel on the beach, so that I can swim and soak up some sun at the same time. Boy, does that sound great! See, my folks aren't the only world travelers. Their only son and his wife get around, too.

Tonight we are (get this) expecting a mortar attack. Tomorrow is election day over here, and the Viet Cong are supposed to stir up trouble to waive the elections. I doubt they will. I hope they don't. I have been mortared, and it shakes me up. I just can't get used to the idea of being shot at. I guess it's a flaw in my character. It probably has something to do with my early upbringing.

I shall close for now. I have been praying about the trip and about seeing you again. If it's His Will, it will come about. I am sure glad He does my worrying for me.

Be good. Remember, I love you very much. And hold your breath; it won't be much longer now.

AML,

J.

Be patient with me, lover. I may not write much, but as each day goes by, closer to Hawaii, I think and dream about you more and more. And when I think of next April, then I really get shook. Just thinking that we will actually be together in our own apartment with our own furniture, and nothing to do but get on each other's nerves. Do you think you will be able to stand it?

Well, really, Angel, I must quit for now. I am sorry you didn't get anything from me on our anniversary. But when you get this, just remember that tomorrow as we pass the date, once again separated by thousands of miles, that I will be thinking of you constantly and of the love I have for you, and thanking God from the bottom of my heart for letting me meet and marry one as great as you.

Keep loving me, because without that I am little more than an empty shell.

All my love,

J.

P.S. Snipers penetrated our perimeter last night, and one soldier was killed. He had no reason to go looking for "Charley" because there is a set plan on how to go about it. But he tried to be a hero, or else just felt it was his duty. And he got shot through the shoulder, and the bullet buried in his chest. He was dead on arrival.

The general waste of lives over here is really getting to me.

J.

The following letter was written to John's parents, Jack
and Muriel Cochrane, on 15 October 1966, 2300 hours. They
received it after they were notified of John's death. Portions of the letter were read by President Lyndon Johnson
when he turned on the Christmas lights at the White House
that year. It has been carried in many newspapers and read
by thousands of people.

Dear Folks:

*Three years ago today on the 15th of October 1963, your son
took upon himself a helpmate. This was one of the smartest things
I've ever done. Two years ago today I was in OCS sweating and
straining for a commission in this man's Army. Last year I was in
Panama sleeping in the jungle and playing games. This 15th of
October, I am sorry to say, I am still in the jungle, but this time the
jungle of Vietnam, and they are not playing games.*

*Tonight, believe this or not, I am awaiting an attack. Yes,
that's right. I kid you not. Your only son who you didn't raise to be
stupid is 11,000 miles from home, sitting here beneath a shaded
Coleman lantern on top of a hill awaiting a visit from friend "Charley". Why I am here I don't know. Well, yes I do, but it doesn't
make me unafraid or untouchable. I am here because it's where I
belong, and because (even though I hate to admit it) I asked to be
here. Not here in this very spot, or even in this country, but because I raised my hand and said, "Yes, Sam, I will do my bit for
wife, family, and Mom's apple pie."*

*Now here I sit so afraid that my stomach is a solid knot, yet
laughing, joking, kidding around with the eighteen troops with
me. I'm even writing a letter to my folks back home as if I hadn't a
care in the world. What I really want to do is load up these men
into the three armored personnel carriers (APC's) we have and get
out of here. I don't belong here. Neither do these men. This isn't*

our war. Why should we have to fight somebody else's war? It doesn't make sense. I refuse to believe that God created a human being and let him live for twenty years just to send him to some foreign land to die at the whim of a skinny Chinese with a long white beard. Surely He had better plans for those whom He made in "His own image."

Why do we have to continually fight? Why do the teachers in our schools preach the glory of wars? Why should they not teach instead the gory side of war—of the thousands upon thousands of lives that have been given up for a flimsy principle or the whim of some politician? Maybe if they could show the hideous and callous side of war, then maybe every little Johnny wouldn't grow up waiting to go to war like his dad. Maybe then people like myself wouldn't be sitting around scared so that we can't even sleep or eat.

It doesn't work. I have considered every excuse in the book, but I know why I am here and why I couldn't be any other place. The reason is because I do believe we should be here, and I do believe that basic principles are enough for a man to die for. Too many people die or take their lives for no good reason, because they are bored or because they can't cope with life any more. At least the soldier knows why he is here, even me; we are here because we actually believe that our country is good enough to fight for, and even, if necessary, die for. All we ask is that some good come out of it. We are also here because we know that if we didn't fight here, then we would be fighting in San Francisco, or New York, or any number of smaller towns in our country. Maybe not in our lifetime, because the politicians could probably talk long enough and hard enough to hold it off for another thirty years or so, but what about our kid's lifetime or their kid's lifetime?

We have our troubles in America, but the little of the world I have seen doesn't hold a candle to our country. Now you may think this is all written in a highly emotional state, and if fear is considered a highly emotional state, and it is, then you are right. But I have sat here this night and looked in the faces of eighteen young men, the oldest is twenty eight, and I have talked to them about their homes and families and wives and sweethearts, and I cannot believe that these men who feel things so strongly could be deceived by propaganda or by a first-class snow job. Every one of these kids knows what he wants.

There is not a hero in the group over here looking for glory or medals or any of that other garbage. They are here because they felt they were needed, that's all. They all have plans; plans that have been put off for a year while they do their bit. Only two of them are "career" soldiers. The rest are just citizen soldiers who have stepped out from the crowd to do what they can. I have had to direct them about what action they should take if "Charley" does pay us a call, and I have had to tell them that once it starts, there can be no giving up. There can be no relenting even if it's to the last man because of the information they have had access to. And as I told them this, they just sat and looked at me, and I could read on their faces the fear, the doubts, and the anger because they are here, and anger because their conscience and personal principles wouldn't let them be any place else.

As they asked the questions, I could feel the tension they were feeling as they asked me what they should do, or where the machine guns should be employed. And I was scared, not because of death, because I have accepted the Lord and I know where I will spend eternity, but because I also had to assume the responsibility for eighteen other lives, and that takes lots of guts. Other people can do it and not even bat an eye. They just say, "The mission came first. What of men as long as the mission is accomplished." And they are right. But what about at night just before they drop off to sleep and they are alone with just themselves and God. What do they say then? Do they still talk about the mission and the job coming first? Or do they ask God to soothe their conscience and forgive them for acting like Him, deciding who will live and who will die.

Tomorrow, if "Charley" doesn't come, this is going to seem kind of silly. But now, right now, it's not. As far as we know, he is coming. All precautions have been taken and double checked. If he comes, he will have a fight on his hands. If he doesn't come, then we will all walk around with sheepish looks on our faces telling those around us that we really weren't afraid. But it's not tomorrow; it's right now, and it's dark, and he is out there. We can hear him. He cannot be laughed off or forgotten about because he is there. If he waits until tomorrow, we will have more men and more weapons here. But is that going to change how we feel now? It is times like right now that we search our souls and are able to see our faults and shortcomings. Tomorrow or the next time it will not be the same. The fear will be there, but then we will be able to look back on this time and say, "We made it then, and we'll make it now!" But now it is the first time for most of these guys. They are new in the country, and even though I have been in similar circumstances since I have been here, none were like they are now. Here I am alone; only I can make the decision. I have to be right. If I am not, then many men may die—good men, men with families and girlfriends and mothers and fathers. What of them? They will get a nice sizeable check from the government, but does that pay for a life? Does that further the principles the man died for? I think not, and that's the real tragedy of this whole stupid situation.

It's now almost 1230 and there is no moon, and the only light is from this lantern and from the work lights on the truck. We are shielded from view and "Charley" knows we are here; the same as we know he is there. I can move from where I am about fifty feet and look down into a valley thick with VC, and we pound the place with artillery and send out small patrols, yet still he is there. It is almost as if he is able to disappear and then reappear again. He is a good soldier. That makes him a formidable enemy. He is fighting this war for principles, also. However, I feel he is wrong, so I kill him if I get the chance because he does not agree with me. That is what this war is all about. A simple disagreement. Yet, we, the most civilized of God's creatures, have to resort to shooting and killing to settle this simple disagreement. Reminds me of that passage from Psalms, "What is man that thou art mindful of him?" That may not be exactly correct and may even be out of context, but the thought is still there. It really seems as if God has turned His back on mankind when one is in a situation like this. With all the intellect and intelligence and scientific discovery He has endowed man with, it boils down to two soldiers on opposite sides, sworn to kill each other because science, intellect, and intelligence could not settle the difference.

This is long and rambling, but it has helped me release a lot of tension. I am going to take one last look around, and then I am going to try to get some sleep. If all goes well, I will finish this tomorrow. Thank goodness that I can call on God at a moment like this.

Until tomorrow, much love,

J.

It is morning. We lasted through the night. There was sniper fire and one or two bursts of automatic weapons, but we survived through the night. I just talked to my CO. Reinforcements are on the way; people who know their business and accept their responsibilities with no fear or panic.

As I have said this morning, a Sunday morning, the troops are going around with a silly grin on their faces, mocking the fear that had gripped them so hard last night. It's over now, and they know it. The front that each of us puts up to hide our inner feelings is once again in place. I have put the word out that reinforcements are on the way, and we will be able to move back to camp when they arrive. Laughter, the thing that was plainly missing last night, is heard now. Man is now back into his element. He can see what is going on around him. He would go into battle during daylight much the same as he would do any other job. But at night, like last night, even if there are a hundred of you, you are alone — just the soldier and the dark and the unknown enemy.

I am still undecided if I will mail this. I feel that last night's experience taught me a great deal. I know I will never get over the fear of possible battle or get used to being the one who decides the life or death of those under me. But during all the excitement of last night, I was able to think clearly and make decisions that had to be made. Only you, my parents, actually know what thoughts I had.

Even now as we sit around eating our C ration breakfast, you can see the men looking at one another and the question is there. Was Jim, Joe, or Sam as afraid as I was? Did my fear show? Will I be looked down upon because I was afraid?

If we could retain the same frankness in our dealings with our fellow man that the 19 of us shared last night, then the world would be a better place. When I see men as I see these men now, I wonder if I will ever know what makes man work. What causes him to do the things he does?

It's a beautiful morning! The sun has just burned away the mist that covered the area when the sun came up. There are things to be done now, so I had better get going.

Continue to pray for me daily as I do you. And kiss all the kids for me.

Love,

J.

My last letter from John dated, 19 October 1966, 2005 hours, Long Binh, Vietnam:

My Dearest Wife:

Only eleven more days, and I will see you again. It's getting closer every second. Matter of fact, it's getting almost too close for anybody to foul up. Boy, is it going to be good to leave here, even if it is only for six days. I just dread the thought of coming back. How about that? Here I haven't even gone, and I am dreading coming back already. I guess I am just hopeless.

I am over the hill now. As a matter of fact, I went under halfway on our anniversary. I left the States on 15 April 1966, so I have to be back on 14 April 1967, which is only 176 days away. Oh, glorious day that will be!

I received a really nice letter from Chuck the other day. He talked about Captain Stallings getting hit and a few other things. Your brother and I think almost alike. I am going to like being able to visit him. Of course, he has always been a great guy to me, even before we were married. (Were we ever not married?)

On our anniversary night I was atop Hill 265 four klicks from Xuan Loc, about twenty six kilometers from here. And believe it or not, I was up there because they thought "Charley" was going to attack. All he did was snipe at us and throw a few grenades our way. But we had APCs (armored personnel carriers) with us, and each of them has three machine guns, and old "Charley" didn't even want to mess with them. It was quite a night. I wrote you and my folks a letter. I mailed the one to my folks, but I burned yours. It was too morbid. It was as if I had expected someone to find it on my dead body the next morning. It was filled with incoherent ramblings about how I felt at the moment and the reasons for my decisions that night. I was scared, that was the problem, and if I was killed or any of the men were, I wanted you to know I had done my best, etc., etc.

However, the Lord watched over me again, and all nineteen of us came through it alright. And for that I shall be eternally thankful. The way the sniper fire was going, it's a miracle that some of us weren't hit. I swore they would never put me in a situation like that again. The last time was with the Australians back in August. But then the CO said if they were going to be hit, "I want you with them." And I fully agreed because I put them out there and wanted to be with them. Don't get me wrong. I wasn't looking for the battle. I just wanted to be sure that everything had been done that could possibly be done. It had been. And we did just a bit more. I sat up all night with a machine gun across my knees and grenades pinned to my flak jacket. If they got me, I wasn't going alone.

But, Angel, I was scared. More so than I have ever been before. It wasn't death that scared me; it was the eighteen other lives I was responsible for. I sometimes think an officer's job is the hardest in the world, if he is conscientious and does his best. I hope I am.

So anyway, I had an exciting anniversary. Not quite the excitement I had in mind, but then I'll make that up in eleven days.

I finally received the honey and nut bread, but the nut bread was moldy so I couldn't eat it. Instead, I have been eating the honey on crackers and drinking the iced tea. It's good. The pause that refreshes and all that!

Say, lover, I know you're going to flip when I say this, but I am thinking of getting a new car over here. I would really like to get a smaller car, like a Corvette or an MG or an Austin Healey or something like that. (Boy, can I dream.) But, really, we should try to sell what we have now. I'll go broke buying gas for it.

Well, lover, this isn't much of a letter but, other than being sniped at a bit more than usual, and working longer and harder hours (I didn't think that was possible), there really isn't a whole heck of a lot going on over here. And I am getting pretty sick of it.

Just a thought. If I weren't married, and I decided to stay in the Army, I'd stay over here. It's because this is the one place in the world that the Army is actually being employed as it should. I am not talking about the killing or the maiming. I am talking about guys like me who are doing a job that counts. And having some pretty good results. Not as good as it could be—but getting better each day. It's a good place for a soldier to learn his trade. Fortunately, I am married, and I am planning on getting out. So Vietnam means nothing to me now but 176 days to sweat it out and leave.

Again, I am going to close. If I don't stop thinking about seeing you in eleven days, I will never be able to make it to the plane. I am losing sleep just thinking about it and would probably sleep through the plane taking off and miss it. But never fear, I could miss anything and everything that happens for the next eleven days, but I'm not about to miss that. I am looking forward to lying around the beach, soaking up some sun, just slightly less than I am looking forward to standing in the airport watching you walk toward me. I shall be one happy man at that time. As a matter of fact, it will be the happiest moment for me since I kissed you good-bye on that lousy pier in San Diego. Remember to keep loving me and know also that as I drop off to sleep every night, my last thoughts are of you.

All my love,
    J.

9

The Worst Possible News

It wouldn't be long now before John and I would be together again! I bought new clothes and was in the process of deciding what to pack. I contacted John's dad in Michigan who was now in the travel business part time, to see if he could make arrangements for my airline tickets. He said he would be glad to help me out. He'd also made arrangements for our hotel in Hawaii. Everything was in place; now I just had to wait to board the plane.

My life was about to change forever, and the news arrived on October 24, 1966. The tall Army officer from Fort Irwin had been selected to notify the next of kin. He was a first lieutenant, the same rank as John, and the message was short: "I've come to bring you the worst possible news I could bring. Your husband, 1st Lt. John Cochrane, was killed by a sniper's bullet this morning in Vietnam. You will be notified shortly by Army officials to make final arrangements." He offered his condolences and in a few minutes was gone. I was left stunned, tearful, and an emotional wreck. How could this be? My suitcase was half packed, my airline ticket was on my dresser, the hotel reservations had been made.

My sister, Emily, called my parents at work. "Come home right away," she told them. "Something has happened to John." When they arrived, I met them at the back door. "John's been killed," I blurted out. They, too, were in stunned disbelief. Everything seemed chaotic. My mom made telephone calls to notify other family members—my sister, Margie, at work; and my brother, Chuck, who was in Chico studying for his Master's Degree. My younger brother, David, would be given the news when he arrived home from school. People from our church were contacted, and the first two people who came to offer their condolences were Mildred Wilson and Ruby Yohn. I remember their hugs and tears of sympathy. They were the first of many, many visitors who came to our home. Within hours, telephone calls, flowers, and cards started arriving. I called my office to inform them of the news, and to say I didn't know how long I would be on leave or when I would be returning to work.

It seemed as if I were in a dream world. I didn't want to fully comprehend or believe what happened. John was gone, that was sure, and there would be no more letters, no reunion in Hawaii, no coming home in April. I'd never feel his arms around me again and never hear him say, "I love you."

John's parents and family in Michigan had to be notified also. We decided to call John's older sister, Pat, and her husband, Rex, and ask them to relay the news to John's parents, Jack and Muriel, and John's other three sisters, Dawn, Jackie, and Sandy. My mom made the call, Rex answered the phone, and Pat picked up an extension from a different room. As mom relayed the message to Rex, she could hear Pat scream in the background. The news was too shocking, too overwhelming.

Muriel was working at Dr. Reuter's office that day. She noticed Rex had come into the doctor's office and gone straight to the back without saying a word to her, and she thought that was rather unusual. Soon Dr. Reuter asked her to step to the back of the office where Rex was waiting.

When she entered the room, he said he had some bad news about John to share with her. At the same time he was saying these words, he was preparing to give her an injection to help cushion the shock of the news she was about to hear. "Oh no, Lord, not John," she cried as she heard the words. John was her only son, and she trusted the Lord to watch over Him and bring him home safely from Vietnam. She knew God made no mistakes, but also knew now she would have to totally depend upon His grace and mercy to see her through the days ahead. She was weak and in shock, but would ask God for His strength; she needed Him now more than ever. She somehow knew He would be there to help in her darkest hour of pain.

John's dad, Jack, was holding a revival in northern Michigan and was playing golf on that Monday morning with some ministers from the area. They noticed a Michigan State Trooper walking toward them on the green. He asked to speak to Reverend Jack Cochrane and told him there had been an emergency, and he would need to return immediately to his home. When Jack asked what the emergency was, the police officer was reluctant to tell him, but upon Jack's insistence was told of John's death. Jack left immediately to return home, and said he didn't remember one thing about the trip, or even how he made it home safely. Family members and friends came together. They consoled each other in their time of grief.

Meanwhile, I was busy making arrangements for the return of John's body. I received a letter from John's commander asking for my permission to allow Lt. Carroll Hughes to escort the body home. I immediately sent word back: "permission granted." I wanted John to be buried in his Army dress blue uniform; I had also requested that his wedding band be buried with him. I was notified that his body would be flown to San Francisco and then on to his home town of Dearborn, Michigan, for the funeral service. The body would then be transferred to Arlington National Cemetery in Arlington, Virginia, for the final resting place. I remembered he had said he wanted to be buried "with all of the war heroes."

I notified 1st Lt. John (Ben) Casey, John's good friend from OCS and Fort Devens, who was stationed in Panama at the time. He immediately caught a flight to California, and I remember him coming from the airport to our house in a taxicab. It was good to see him again, and he planned to accompany me and my family to Michigan for the funeral and to Arlington for the burial. I was happy to hear that he would lend a shoulder for us to lean on. (Ben was also killed in Vietnam in March 1968. He had completed one tour of duty and had extended for an additional six months. He received shrapnel wounds when his company was overrun by the Viet Cong.)

I received the following letter from John's Commanding Officer:

```
DEPARTMENT OF THE ARMY
HEADQUARTERS
303D RADIO RESEARCH BATTALION
APO SAN FRANCISCO, CALIFORNIA 96266

Mrs. John F. Cochrane
6712 Palm Avenue
Highland, California

Dear Elaine:
```

It is with deepest personal regrets that I write to you of John's death on the 24th of October 1966. I am quite unable to convey to you just how profoundly this terrible thing has affected every officer and soldier he knew.

He was reconnoitering an access route from the Squadron base camp about eleven kilometers south of Xuan Loc on Provincial Route #2 to a hill (324) about one kilometer to the north with Captain Lee W. Gentry, Detachment Commander and Acting Sergeant Frederick D. Evans, Team Chief. At 0810 as their vehicle, an M-151 quarter ton truck, slowed to turn off of Provincial Route #2 to climb the hill, a command detonated Claymore mine exploded about fifteen feet to its right front, with most of the charge going over the top of the windshield. At the same time, four rounds of sniper fire hit the front of the vehicle, one of which went through the passenger side windshield and struck John. All three passengers dove or fell out of the vehicle. Captain Gentry's first act was to check to see how badly John had been hurt, but he had already passed away. Both medical and combat support personnel arrived immediately and evacuated Captain Gentry and John to the 93d Evacuation Hospital at Long Binh. Captain Gentry was treated for multiple minor facial wounds and returned to duty the same day. The driver was not wounded.

Chaplain (Major) Thomas F. Egan, 11th Armored Cavalry Regimental Chaplain, not knowing John's religious affiliation, provisionally ministered the last rites of the Catholic Church, as he was the only chaplain in the area at the time. A memorial service was held at 0800, 27 October 1966, at the Regimental Headquarters Chapel by Father Egan and Chaplain (Major) Dalton H. Barnes, the regiment's Protestant chaplain to give all those officers and soldiers with whom he was acquainted an opportunity to pay their respects. He was loved and respected by these officers and men, and his death has cast a pall over this entire battalion.

For those of us who had worked with John at Battalion Headquarters and were watching him develop into an outstanding platoon leader, the sense of loss is greater because of our close personal regard for him. We will always remember him as a dedicated, professional officer and a warm, outgoing person and friend.

If there is any way that I can be of assistance to you, please let me know, and I and my officers will do our best to provide it.

Please accept the deepest sympathy of the officers and men of the 303d Radio Research Battalion.

John J. Masters
LTC AIS
Commanding

10
Burial at Arlington

Now we had to decide which family members would make the trip to Michigan for John's funeral. My parents, of course, would go. They loved John like a son, my dad always said. My sister, Emily, and fifteen year old brother, David, would also be on board when the flight took off. My grandmother lived with us at the time so my sister, Margie, volunteered to stay home with her. My brother, Chuck, was unable to make the trip, but he loved John, too. He would be there with us in thoughts and prayer.

The church I attended in San Bernardino, California, held a memorial service for John on the Sunday after he died but, unfortunately, our family had already left for Michigan. After the pastor gave an appropriate message, he closed the service with a prayer for the family and for the soldiers still fighting in Vietnam. He read the following poem written by Austin W. Conklin:

God's Way Is Best

> I know not where my Lord may lead—
> O'er barren plain or grassy mead;
> Through valley or on mountain crest;
> But where He leads, I know 'tis best.
>
> I know not what a day may bring
> Of perfect health or suffering;
> Of rich delight, or deep distress,
> Keen disappointment or success.

Nor do I know at morning sun
If life shall last til day is done.
But this I know, come toil or rest,
God always sends me what is best.

And when life's evening shadows fall,
And I shall hear the final call,
I'll lean my head upon His breast,
And say, "Dear Lord, Thy way is best."

The funeral service for John was held at First Baptist Church of Wayne, Michigan, on November 1, 1966, 2:30 p.m. Many, many friends came by to offer their condolences and sympathy, including several close friends who had attended school with John. I also notified Lt. Lee Carroll, one of John's close friends from OCS, who drove several hundred miles to pay his respects.

Pastor Larry Coy conducted the service. I remember some words from one of the songs."It's not where I wish to go, or what I wish to be...." This path was definitely not one I would have chosen. I, too, would need to lean heavily upon Him to see me through. It wasn't going to be easy; this I knew. The church provided a lovely dinner after the service where I met several of John's friends and family members, some for the first time. It was evident that John was loved by his family and friends.

We all drove by caravan to Arlington National Cemetery for the burial ceremony with full military honors. I received word that two wives, whose husbands were in the same battalion with John in Vietnam, planned to attend the ceremony and would meet us at Arlington. One was the wife of Capt. James Stallings, killed in action just a month earlier. She knew the pain I was feeling. It would be good to see her again.

Family members were picked up at the hotel and driven to the cemetery in a black limousine. It was rainy and overcast, and the raindrops splashing on the windows made the outside world a dark blur passing in slow motion. There was little said inside the limousine; each of us was lost in our own thoughts. When we arrived at the starting point of the funeral procession, I noticed the horse-drawn caisson with John's flag-draped casket aboard, and the riderless horse depicting a warrior lost in battle. What an awesome sight! Everything was done in such a precise and perfect manner. *John would be proud*, I thought. As we proceeded through the winding streets, we saw white tombstones as far as the eye could see. They stood as a solemn reminder of the thousands who had paid the supreme sacrifice so that we might walk free. I remembered a Bible verse from the book of John, "Greater love hath no man than this, that a man lay down his life for his friends."

People walking through the cemetery stepped quickly to the side in hushed silence to let the procession through. A look of sympathy was on their faces, and their eyes were full of questions. The Vietnam War truly was a controversial war. It was a war we didn't understand, and it was lasting too long and taking too many lives. Over 58,000 lives would eventually be lost before it was over. Was the price too high? How can we put a price on freedom? It is truly a precious gift bought by those who have given their lives.

The steel-gray, flag-draped casket was now in place, and flowers were everywhere. The chaplain was standing at the head of the casket speaking words of comfort, life, and hope. This was not the end; we knew we would see John again. John even spoke of that in one of his letters when he said, "I'm not afraid of death because I have accepted the Lord, and I know where I will spend eternity." And each of us who are Christians have that same hope within us.

The soldiers stood tall as they folded the flag ever so gently and with perfect precision. It was presented to me with a few short words of gratitude and thanksgiving for one who was willing to give his all. The 21-gun salute rang out loud and clear, and the lone soldier sounded taps from a nearby hill. The soldiers quickly carried the casket from the awning-covered area to its final resting place. The funeral with full military honors was now over.

B. Clarke King, a family friend, wrote the following account of the burial ceremony:

The leaves were tumbling lazily down out of a low sky painted dull gray by the overhanging clouds. The tent had been raised to protect a small area from the softly falling rain. It was a small area, just large enough for a dozen or so people and the casket. The casket represented the highest debt a person can pay for his beliefs, evidenced by the American flag on top, the chaplain at the head of it, and the look on his mother's face.

He had been a good boy, raised in a fine family with love and faith, and he sometimes wondered if the things he was involved in in Vietnam was worth all the good that was supposed to come of it.

The chaplain prayed, the soldiers fired three volleys, and the bugler's notes were clear, but sad as taps sounded from a distant hilltop. The flag was folded so perfectly, ever so gently, and with respect. My heart was heavy as I watched his mother. She was a strong woman, watching her only son laid to rest, so full of grief and yet reserved.

The chaplain's words went mostly unheard; oh the gist of them registered, but the words were anticipated. Instead, the mother's thoughts were miles apart and years away. He was an infant boy, then suddenly a young man who confided in her as she shared his disappointments and anxieties, ups and downs. In her own hopes and dreams she trained and guided him, and for what? I could almost hear her asking, "God, why?" and then begging Him for forgiveness because as a human she had difficulty understanding His judgment. For a moment it was ever so quiet. Maybe it was the soft rain, maybe it was...well...who knows?

As I looked around to break the spell, I saw the white horses pulling the now empty black wagon over a hill in the distance. In the foreground were the soldiers and their rifles, standing patiently waiting and glad they were in America and not in Vietnam. The crowd in the distance started breaking up and moving on as we all started back to our cars. As we left the curb, the workmen started to lower the casket that was surrounded by flowers. The rain would keep them fresh for a few days. Other workmen were already taking down the tent. It was just another day for them.

As we drove through Arlington Cemetery past the thousands of white crosses, I wondered just how many families and friends had stood here in the past and shared the same sadness I saw on each face today. Far to the west the sun was shining through. Tomorrow would be a better day, but, for the moment, the rain was still falling, and the leaves were tumbling lazily down, to rest forever.

We returned to the black limousine for our return ride through the winding streets of Arlington. President Lyndon Johnson would later say, as he read John's last letter to his parents, "I have known many brave men and wise men, but I wish I had known 1st Lt. John F. Cochrane. Then I would have known the best of men."

And he was right.

***

Upon hearing of John's death, Capt. T.J.M. Richards of the Australian Forces, Vietnam sent the following letter to John's parents:

Dear Mr. & Mrs. Cochrane:

As John may have mentioned in his letters, we worked together for six weeks in August and September 1966. During that time, he and I lived in the same tent and came to know each other well. We shared our dreams, hopes, faith, aspirations, and ambitions.

Perhaps the finest compliment that Australian soldiers can pay any man to demonstrate that he is an equal, is to call him "mate" and tease him mercilessly. John was paid this compliment very soon after his arrival, and, when he reciprocated the friendship, helped to further cement the respect in which he was held.

If ever you and your family visit Australia, please remember that there are sixteen Aussies who would be only too pleased to make your acquaintance, "shout you a beer," and say, "Owyergoin' Mate, arright?" To a friendship formed in adversity and which will always be remembered.

Yours sincerely,
Trevor Richards

President Lyndon Johnson addressing wounded Vietnam veterans during the turning on of the Christmas lights at the White House in 1966. President Johnson read a portion of John's last letter written to his parents.

11

Healing

It has now been many years since John died, and since that time I have experienced many peaks and valleys in my life. The day finally came when I was set free from the deep depression and fears that held me captive for so long. Actually, when the release came it seemed such a simple thing. For many years, I had asked ministers to pray for me: "I want to be free on the inside, free from the doubts and fear attacking my mind. Please pray for me." The depression became chronic. I went to work and led a seemingly normal life, but inside the spiritual war raged on, and I couldn't find freedom no matter how I struggled. There was some relief along the way, but it wasn't until the 1980s that God touched my mind and life and set me free.

I had been reading a book about positive imaging, and there were three words in the book that caught my attention, "Act as if." When you pray, "act as if" your prayer is heard, and, more important, "act as if" it's been answered. It was like a light going on inside my head, but it seemed so simple. My life had been dominated by feelings for so long, and I now realized I had to forget how I felt and start walking in what I believed. We operate in this physical world by our five senses, but in the spiritual world it's just the opposite. We believe before our senses tell us it's true. Faith and feelings don't mix. Hadn't the Bible clearly stated that when you pray you must believe that your prayer is answered before you see it manifested in the physical realm? Why had it taken me so long to realize this for myself?

I prayed a simple prayer: "God, I can't live like this any more, and I ask you to set me free. If you can't or won't set me free, then please take me to heaven to be with you." It wasn't that I wanted to die, I just couldn't live without His presence in my life any more. I couldn't live with the fears and doubts that plagued me night and day. I couldn't "just snap out of it," or "just think positive," as some had suggested. Something had a hold on my life, and I couldn't get free.

I had invited Jesus into my life when I was a young girl, and I remember how new and clean I felt inside. The grass looked greener, and the sky looked bluer than I had ever remembered. I felt like a brand new person. And that's what the Bible said would happen when we invite Him into our life; we become a "new creature." But somewhere along the way something happened in my life. I realized Christians are in a spiritual warfare and have a spiritual enemy by the name of Satan, and he's out to destroy us. But I thought he was out to destroy someone else, not me. The Bible teaches that Satan is a liar and the father of lies, and his tactics haven't changed since he deceived Eve in the Garden of Eden. He had planted doubt in her heart and mind when he said, "You shall not surely die?" I didn't realize the mind was the battlefield and how important it is to guard our thought life. Thoughts were attacking my mind, and I took them in, believed them, and dwelled on them as if they were my own thoughts. I didn't realize they were lies from Satan, and they became strongholds in my life.

I ended my prayer with, "Dear Lord, I believe you have heard and answered my prayer, and I will begin thanking you now even before the answer comes." Within hours of praying that prayer, something wonderful happened. For the first time in years my mind was free. I was free on the inside. The fears and depression were gone. In it's place, I could sense God's presence again, His powerful and wonderful presence in my life once more. I was free, and faith—little though it was—had made the difference!

Of course, we Christians are all in a spiritual warfare, and that warfare will continue until we leave this earth. The Lord set me completely free when I prayed, but, of course, Satan still tries to bring fear, anxiety, and depression upon me, but the Lord has brought me to victory every time. It's good to know that the Lord didn't leave us helpless and hopeless on this earth. He left us an instruction book—the Bible—and in that book He tells us that He has made every provision for us so that we can have victory in every area of our lives. It's up to us to appropriate what He's done for us. Through the Bible He says, "Don't wait for Me to come down and move in your circumstances. I'm waiting for you to stand up and walk in what is already yours."

The year following John's death I remarried. I didn't like being a widow and alone, and I wanted to find the happiness I had had with John. I didn't ask God to lead me to the one He had for me; I just plunged ahead and made my own decisions and did not wait for guidance from Him. Unfortunately, the marriage ended in a divorce a few years later. I continued to try to put the pieces of my life back together again, but nothing seemed to fit. I ended up marrying again, and that marriage too ended in divorce within three short years.

However, from that marriage nearly thirty years ago, God gave me a beautiful daughter, my only child, and she has truly been a blessing sent from God. My sister, Emily, gave me some advice, "You need to learn to wait—wait for what God has planned for your life. That's the only way you'll find happiness again." That's the best advice I've ever had. I've been patient, and God is putting the pieces of my life back together again.

My daughter recently moved out of state to attend graduate school, and I took an early retirement from work. At that time I said, "God, here I am. Can you use me?" And from somewhere deep within me, I heard Him say, "Follow me." I am now looking forward to the most exciting time of my life—to be used by the Master. I can't wait to see what He has in store!

At John's gravesite,
Arlington National Cemetery

Epilogue

1st Lt. John Cochrane was posthumously awarded the Bronze Star, the Army Commendation Medal, and the Purple Heart. The medals were presented to his widow, Elaine Cochrane, and his mother, Muriel Cochrane, at Fort MacArthur, San Pedro, by Col. Mark Brennan, the Commanding Officer at Fort MacArthur.

The Bronze Star citation reads:

"1st Lt. Cochrane's outstanding achievements and devotion to duty, at the cost of his life, were in keeping with the highest traditions of the military service and reflect great credit upon himself, his unit, and the U.S. Army."

The citation for the Army Commendation Medal reads:

"Through his outstanding professional competence and devotion to duty he consistently obtained superior results. Working long and arduous hours, he set an example that inspired his associates to strive for maximum achievement. His performance was in the best traditions of the U.S. Army and reflects great credit upon himself and the military service."

1st Lt. Cochrane was also posthumously awarded the National Order Medal, Fifth Class and the Gallantry Cross with Palm by the Government of the Republic of Vietnam.

The following article was carried in the *San Bernardino Sun Newspaper* in the "Voice of the People" column:

In your issue of the *Evening Telegram*, November 28, 1966, there was an article about 1Lt John Cochrane of Highland. He was killed here in Vietnam fighting for his country and leading the men he was commanding. In the article was a letter written to his parents. We have a copy of this letter, and it is posted for the use of the whole unit. The night Lt. Cochrane wrote that letter I was one of the eighteen men with him. Lt. Cochrane will always be the bravest man I'll ever meet. He was the best officer I have ever known.

SP-4 Roger W. Boyd
409th Radio Research Det.
11th Armored Cavalry Regiment
APO San Francisco 96257

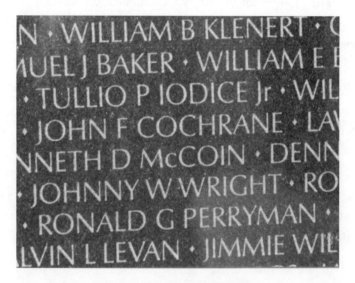

"From Vietnam to the Wall"

Order Form

Postal orders:
Elaine Cochrane Murphy, P.O. Box 135, Patton, CA 92369

Telephone orders: (909) 862-1831

Please send *Dearest Angel* **to:**

Name:_____

Address:_____

City:_____ State:_____

Zip:_____

Telephone: (_____) _____

Book Price: $10.00 in U.S. dollars.

Sales Tax: Please add 8.25% for books shipped to a California
address.

Shipping: $4.00 for the first book and $1.00 for each additional
book to cover shipping and handling within US,
Canada, and Mexico. International orders add $7.00
for the first book and $3.00 for each additional book.